With the Cavalry in the West

With the Cavalry in the West

The Experiences of a British Hussar Officer
During the First World War

ILLUSTRATED

"Aquila"

LEONAUR

With the Cavalry in the West
The Experiences of a British Hussar Officer During the First World War
by "Aquila"

ILLUSTRATED

First published under the title
With the Cavalry in the West

Leonaur is an imprint of Oakpast Ltd

Copyright in this form © 2020 Oakpast Ltd

ISBN: 978-1-78282-910-2 (hardcover)
ISBN: 978-1-78282-911-9 (softcover)

http://www.leonaur.com

Publisher's Notes

The views expressed in this book are not necessarily
those of the publisher.

Contents

Chapter 1

Sandhurst

It seems like looking up a page of very ancient history when I take my mind back to the day on which I entered Sandhurst. So much has been crammed into those four and a half years that the beginning of them seems to belong to another world. And yet, in a way, they have gone quickly. Time always does fly when you are busy. And it is only since 1914 that I have learnt what it means to be really busy. One thought one had a lot to do in Trial Week at school, or when one was head of this or captain of that. But if necessary, one could do twice the work—I mean if one really had to. At Oxford, where I passed a few pleasant terms, one thought one was busy in school's week; but it seems as nothing compared to what people have had to do since, both in military and civil life. Everyone has been at high pressure.

I had not always been destined for the army, and anyone can imagine the jar of going from the peaceful life of Oxford to Sandhurst. True, I spent some weeks training with a Service Battalion, and this certainly did a little bit to prepare me for the coming shock, but it was only when I appeared late for the first parade that I suddenly awoke to the full meaning of military discipline. Scarcely had I shown myself at the door outside which the company fell in, when there was a roar from Sergeant Biddulph, our staff sergeant, and I was marched off under arrest.

I felt like a person who during a dream rolls out of bed and falls with a crash on to the floor, only waking to the grim reality when he finds that he has a black eye and a bleeding nose. I managed to repeat this performance a few days later, but afterwards I became more or less "broken in," for this time I received such a "telling off" from Captain Dench, our company commander, that I was never late again. I cannot remember all that occurred when I was marched up to orderly room, but it was something like this:

After the evidence had been given by Sergeant Biddulph—who stood as rigid as a door-post on my right—Dench proceeded to address me:

"Sewell, this is the second time in a week that you have been brought before me for being late on parade."

"Yes, sir."

"You will have the goodness to remember that you are no longer a civilian."

"Yes, sir."

"You are a soldier, or, shall I say, I shall do my best to make you one."

"Yes, sir."

"The first thing you must do is to give up these slovenly habits: look at your boots, man, they are not even clean. Just smarten yourself up a bit, young man. Staff sergeant, you will keep a special eye on Mr. Sewell, do you see?"

"Yes, sir."

"If there is any more trouble with you, young man, you will go before the commandant. As it is, you will do seven days' restriction. March out!"

I have often noticed how hard it is to perform the simplest drill movement in an orderly room. I suppose it is the atmosphere of the place that turns one into an idiot. On this occasion, when Sergeant Biddulph said "Right turn!" I turned to the left and cannoned into my escort. Then followed more abuse, and I left Bench's presence sadder and wiser.

Bench put the "wind up" us all. He was a severe-looking man with extraordinarily piercing eyes. He showed no mercy to the slackers, although he was always ready to help the more backward of us. He was absolutely fair and favoured nobody. Off parade he was quite a different being. Occasionally we used to go down to tea and dinner at his house in the town, and he did all kinds of things for us. Naturally he was liked and admired by everyone.

Before the war there had been only infantry companies at Sandhurst. Now, however, there was in addition a cavalry company with special instructors.

"K" Company consisted of about sixty cadets, and we were divided into three troops, each in a different stage of training. Our troop was commanded by Captain Black. He was thoroughly up to date in his knowledge, and was a very keen soldier in every way. He was a first-rate instructor, and appeared to take an immense amount of trouble over us. That is what people like; everyone loves to feel that someone else is taking a real interest in him.

Reveille was at 6 a.m., when bugles were sounded in every part of the building. In addition to this a man used to come round with a huge stick, and bang loudly on every door. At 6.55 we used to fall in for riding school, the roll was called and we marched down to the stables.

For riding school, we were divided into two "rides" of ten, each under a separate instructor. The riding instructors were all sergeants specially selected as being suitable to train cadets. My ride was under Sergeant Ullathorne of the 19th Hussars. I think that he was one of the best instructors I have ever come across. He was a man who seemed to understand how to treat cadets. He had a strong sense of discipline and he did his best to instil this into us.

I should say that Sandhurst Cadets are the most difficult people in the world to manage. We used to take all the liberties we could and it needed a firm hand to manage us. Sergeant Ullathorne did it in just the right way. He knew at once if you were not doing your best, and he used to point out the fact with some asperity. His abuse was usually terse and to the point, but occasionally, when we were particularly stupid, he would stand in the middle of the school with his hands on his hips and abuse the whole lot of us *en bloc*.

"Upon my word, gentlemen," he would say, "I think you are the most vacant lot it 'as ever been my luck to 'andle. There don't seem to be one of yer as 'as got the remotest idea 'ow to 'andle a 'orse. There yer goes again, Mr. Cunningham; what the 'ell are yer 'angin' over that 'orse's 'ead for? You're off, sir, you're right off. I told yer so. When you goes over a jump yer knows perfectly well what to do, only yer won't do it. You ain't fit to ride a rockin'-'orse, much less a cavalry 'orse. If the captain was to come in now, 'e would send yer to the infantry; and 'e'd be right too. There ain't one of yer what really rides yer 'orse. Yer just jogs around like lumps of coal on a shovel. Sit up, Mr. Delius, for 'eaven's sake; yer looks just like an old man of eighty, or a wet sack. Yer goin' into the cavalry not into the camel corps. Yer enough to break any instructor's 'eart."

We were treated to a harangue of this kind every few days. Sergeant Ullathorne's vocabulary was astonishing. He never used the same word twice.

Everyone was asked whether he had ever ridden before, or ever hunted. It was far better to say no to both these questions, because if the instructors thought that you fancied yourself, they gave you a very thin time. I am not ashamed to say that I did fancy myself. I had ridden ever since I was seven years old, and was not a little piqued at being asked whether I had ever been on a horse before. I therefore answered both the questions in the affirmative. I was sorry for it afterwards, for Sergeant Ullathorne made things exceedingly unpleasant for me.

The worst horseman of the lot was Cunningham. In riding school, he usually rode just in front of me. His seat was really appalling. He used to roll about from side to side just like an egg on a spoon. Sergeant Ullathorne used to compare him to a duck in a thunderstorm, a ship in a rough sea, and various other things.

However, although his qualities as a horseman were not great, he became a splendid soldier, and now holds the M.C. and bar and has been mentioned in despatches. I think he came in for

"You ain't fit to ride a rockin'-'orse, much less a cavalry 'orse."

more abuse than anyone else in the ride. Captain Sykes, the riding master, also had a go at him, but no one seemed to bring about much improvement.

The first few lessons were, of course, "cushy." No one fell off or made an exhibition of himself. But things soon became more exciting. We were trotted round without stirrups or reins for something like half an hour out of each lesson. Once I fell off from sheer exhaustion of the riding muscles. After getting on again we were put over a gorse and wood hurdle, first with reins and stirrups and then without either.

On the latter occasion my horse refused, after galloping up to the hurdle, and shot me about twenty yards over the obstacle. I must have landed on my head, for I remember nothing more until I found myself sitting in a corner of the riding school with the instructors standing round me asking whether the standard of horsemanship out hunting in my part of the country was not somewhat lower than in most parts. Then I regretted not having said that I had never ridden before. I advise everyone to say that. It is wiser.

Riding without stirrups is very trying at first, but it is a most necessary evil, since it is the only way to acquire strength in the thighs. After about a week you get quite used to it; I soon even felt more secure over a jump without stirrups than with them.

As we became more advanced, we did other mounted training. It takes a good horseman to ride a semi-trained horse over jumps without wings. This we had to do—first holding the reins with both hands, and later with the reins in one hand and a sword in the other. On one occasion I made a fearful exhibition of myself. My horse pecked at a jump, but at the last minute the brute decided to go over it. His leap was so sudden that I was jerked out of the saddle on to his neck. I lost both stirrups, besides the reins. Seeing my discomfiture, the brute started off at full gallop round the paddock; he took one fence of his own free will, and then increased his pace until it must have approached to something like Derby rate. During this performance I was still on his neck with my arms round his throat. In my position it was useless to attempt to stop his mad career, so I decided to sit tight and let him do his worst.

Both instructors and cadets were too astounded by this grotesque spectacle to do anything, and I had been twice round the field before anyone made a move.

Suddenly there was a roar like that of an infuriated bull, and I realised that Captain East had arrived and was taking the situation in hand. Everyone now shouted different advice, none of which I was able to follow. I saw a number of people rushing to shut the gate of the paddock, but they were too late. The horse beat the first of them by a head, and away he went *ventre à terre*, past the riding school and into the woods, up one of the many tracks that lead towards Crowthorne and Easthampstead. This stage of the drama only lasted about four minutes as, coming to a sharp rise, the horse slowed down to a canter and I managed to wriggle back into the saddle. After this I easily pulled up. Such was the end of this dramatic ride. I had many experiences of this kind hunting at home, but this was the most exciting I had known.

When we had become more or less competent horsemen, we did a lot of dummy-thrusting with swords, mounted drill and field-days. Dummy-thrusting is great fun; but you must have a horse that does not shy at the dummy. The mark was usually a sack stuffed with straw, on a gallows, or on the ground. We used to go at this at full gallop, and this gave one some idea of the terror that a cavalry charge inspires.

In addition to riding school there were classes in care and fitting of saddlery, grooming, putting on, marching order, veterinary first aid, etc.

We used to have breakfast at eight, and usually a lecture at nine. At eleven there was occasionally a company foot parade, for which our "turn out" had to be absolutely spotless. I have known people get twent-yeight days' restriction for wearing a pin in their collar, and other minor offences. The foot-drill instructors were all Guards' sergeants, and the finest men I have ever seen. All were over six feet in height and most were correspondingly broad.

The drill at Sandhurst before the war was said to have been up to the Guards' standard; now, of course, the time a cadet stayed at the college was much shorter, but I believe that the standard was very nearly as high nevertheless.

Every Saturday there was a battalion parade, that is to say, a parade and march past of the whole college. This performance was usually watched by a number of visitors, and was certainly worth seeing.

After this parade we were free until 11 p.m. One could also get weekend leave, an innovation which was introduced by our company commander.

I am quite certain that one result of the concession, weekend leave, was a great improvement in the work of the cadets during the week. There was plenty of both physical and mental work of all kinds, so that one needed to be absolutely fit to be able to carry it out. Nothing did us more good than to be able to get clean away from the place every now and then.

Monday morning was always rather unpleasant. The before-breakfast hour on that day was always foot-drill of the most violent kind. Most of us were, as a rule, somewhat peevish at the thought of another whole week in front of us, and the drill was usually bad for the first few minutes. Our staff sergeant knew us and our feelings exactly: I think one can only describe this feeling as Monday-morningish.

Sergeant Biddulph had the faculty of dispersing the Monday-morning atmosphere quicker than any man I have ever known. One hears a lot about gouty and liverish old men who are unapproachable before 11 a.m. any day, but I should like to have seen Sergeant Biddulph drill a squad of these as he used to drill us. There would have been a marked improvement in their attitude towards their fellow beings. An hour's marching, double-marching, right-turning, left-turning, about-turning, sloping and ordering arms did one a heap of good, especially when these movements followed each other with such rapidity that sometimes one did not know which way one was facing.

The words of command were accompanied by occasional roars from an assistant staff sergeant who marched in rear of us, and by loud and not infrequent abuse from Captain Dench, who usually attended this parade in none too good a temper himself.

After an hour of this I think everyone felt better; then came breakfast.

One dramatic event took place the very first week I arrived. About 2 a.m. one morning there broke out above my room such a running, shouting and scampering of feet that I surmised something unusual was occurring. The shouting was soon accompanied by blood-curdling yells, hunting noises and cracking of crops; after about a minute the hunt passed down the stairs, and along the passage, past my door and out into the grounds where the "yoicking" and "hallooing" gradually died away. In about ten minutes the hunt returned.

I went to see what the quarry was that they were pursuing at that hour of the morning, and discovered that a fellow in the company who slept above us was to be publicly bathed on account of his alleged reluctance to perform sufficient ablutions when left alone. He had suspected the raid, and made a bolt for it when he heard his assailants coming. They had had a good run, but had outflanked their fox and headed him into a wire fence, where he was pulled down. The whole party were in pyjamas, except the unfortunate fox, who had only the bottom part of his on, the other half having been torn from his back during the chase.

On one occasion an unfortunate fellow, who was rather unpopular, was attacked in the night and his eyebrows were shaved off. I think this was going a bit too far, as they had not grown properly almost a year afterwards. There was considerable trouble over the affair next day, and after this an officer always slept in the house to prevent a recurrence of any further events of this kind.

I will not dwell on the other details of our training. The schemes were quite amusing. These took place sometimes on horses and sometimes on bicycles. I must say that the bicycle-riding was the most violent and erratic that I have ever seen. Very few of the machines had brakes, and I have seen one fellow collapse and bring down six or seven on the top of him through sheer inability on their part to stop. Sandhurst cadets on bicycles have only one speed, that is, top speed. Strange to say I only heard of one or two accidents all the time I was there.

Occasionally we went for long distance schemes, out beyond Harford Bridge, Godalming and other places, but most of our battles took place round Crowthorne, Bagshot, Chobham, Eversley, and within a radius of six or seven miles.

On the day I passed out I made another exhibition of myself in the paddock, and came down horse and all in the presence of Sir James Wolfe Murray and a numerous staff, who had come down from the War Office to inspect us.

About a month before I had been made a corporal, and on frequent occasions commanded a section on field days. There is nothing nicer than having one's own show, whatever be the size of one's command. I shall have something to say about this later on.

Chapter 2

Arrival in France

I will pass over the time I spent with my reserve regiment, and go ahead to the day when I landed in France the following October, bringing with me a draft of a hundred men. We travelled *via* Southampton and Rouen, where we rested twenty-four hours, after which we entrained again for our final destination. My regiment was at this time near Aire, where we arrived at about 4 p.m. the following day. Here I found a guide who brought us to Regimental Headquarters, which were in a large *château* some two miles out of the town, and were distinguished by a lance and pennon stuck into the earth at the main gate. Here my hundred men were taken away by the regimental sergeant-major, an imposing person with a loud voice and a breast full of medals.

After being brought to the colonel and given some tea, I was told that I was to go to "C" Squadron to which I had been posted. This squadron was commanded by Major Stephens, who was, as I soon discovered, a remarkably keen and efficient soldier. I had some tea at Regimental Headquarters before going off with Major Stephens. Unfortunately, the chair on which I sat was a very shaky one, and just as I was pouring out some tea one of the legs gave way and I collapsed on the floor, taking the tea-pot and sundry articles of crockery with me. This was an unfortunate beginning.

Joining a regiment is at all times, I believe, an unpleasant ordeal, at least I had always heard so before the war. I must confess that I had the "wind up" more when I entered the squadron mess than I ever have on any other occasion before or since.

At a time like this you know that everyone is staring at you and is sizing you up. You can almost follow their thoughts. Some, you suppose, are saying to themselves: "Rum-looking bloke, this," or, "I wonder what he's like," or again, "He doesn't look a bad sort."

I must say that my reception was extremely hospitable, and that everyone was extraordinarily nice. Of course, if you have had a father or uncle in the regiment before you it makes things much easier, but when you are unknown and are judged purely on your own merits it is advisable to try to avoid committing any atrocity at first.

Dinner was being served when I arrived, and I was made to sit down at once and feel at home. I was not sorry to get something to eat, since my last meal had been at Rouen the previous evening.

There were six officers in the squadron besides myself, so that I was not to command a troop for the present. I was posted to a troop which was commanded by an officer with a wealth of experience of soldiering both in peace and war. Stephens said that I might imitate him in everything I did, and this I zealously tried to do. Davidson—or "Duff," as he was called—was a fine soldier. He had come out at the beginning of the war, had been through all the early battles of the campaign, and latterly the Battle of Loos, in which cavalry had been employed though with little success. He had an enormous personality, and, I could see, was universally liked and respected.

I was in his troop three weeks before one of the other troop leaders left, and I was promoted in his place. I look upon these three weeks as some of the most precious of my time out here. Duff taught me everything it was possible to teach in that time. He told me all that I needed to know for the moment about billets, horses, saddlery, routine, discipline, etc., and even took me out for tactical rides and gave me some idea of what cavalry can do. A lot of this I had learnt theoretically at Sandhurst; but I believe I learnt more in those three weeks than in many months in England.

I got up at reveille every day, went out to exercise, saw the feeds made out for the horses, the rations for the men, in fact saw everything. Duff was a capital instructor: I only hope I was an apt learner.

The first morning after my arrival I came down to breakfast just in time to hear Stephens having a violent quarrel with the owner of the village forge, who refused to allow us the use of it. This woman was one of the biggest I have ever seen, and had also a remarkably loud voice. Stephens is rather short, but what he lacks in stature he makes up for in energy, for he is one of the most active men I have ever met. The sight of these two engaged in this heated altercation was so comical, that it was as much as I could do to keep a straight face.

The tension was increased by the presence of the squadron sergeant-major, a man with a large moustache and a very fierce red face. He was standing rigid behind the major, apparently unmoved by the grotesque spectacle before him. Eventually the argument ceased through the exhaustion of both parties—I do not know what the result was—and the woman left the house. This affair seemed to upset Stephens somewhat, for he was quite unapproachable all that day.

The village in which we were billeted was by no means uncomfortable. All the horses were under cover, and the men in warm quarters. I was of course immensely interested in what I saw, for this was my first experience of real soldiering. I had always pictured the cavalry officer as a great hulking fellow with a swaggering gait and a loud voice, and never a thought beyond wine and women. I imagined that a pair of breeches from Savile Row and boots from Peal were *sine qua non*, I was relieved to find that this was not the case. It mattered far more what kind of head you had on your shoulders than what pattern of breeches were on your legs, though in peace time I believe fine breeches and boots were thought far more of than a level head.

The officers' mess was a nice room in a farmhouse, for which we paid one *franc* per day. This was not ruinous, and the room was, moreover, extremely comfortable. *Madame* was a dear old thing very different from the lady from the forge over the way. She had copious supplies of milk, eggs and butter and supplied us with these very cheaply.

Ingham was mess-president, and a very good and systematic one. Every evening Corporal Raikes, the mess waiter, brought him the accounts made out in detail, and he ordered lunch and dinner for the next day. The messing was not expensive, and came only to four *francs* a day.

Above the mess was Stephens' bedroom. He always went to bed fairly early and some of the rest of us were usually below playing bridge for some time after he had gone.

About the third night after I had joined, Ingham and some of the others were making a good deal of noise singing to an old piano on which we used to strum. Apparently, the noise was too much for Stephens, for I distinctly heard him rap several times on the floor of his room above us. I do not know whether the others heard it, but at any rate the singing and shouting went on more loudly than before. I had a kind of feeling that a tragedy was about to occur and

I had not long to wait, for suddenly there was a noise as though someone was falling downstairs, the door burst open and the irate major stood in the doorway, clad in pyjamas. He had got out of bed to stop the din which we were making, and which was preventing him from getting to sleep, but in his haste to come downstairs he had fallen down them. This did not increase his good temper. I will not tell you what he said, because most of it is unprintable, but the musical evening came to an end forthwith.

The result of this affair was seen next day.

The squadron paraded for drill at 9 a.m., and the major was in his worst humour. Personally, I did not care, as I was not leading a troop and was only a spectator. But what happened was not without its humorous side. First, he "crabbed" the turn-out of the men, then that of the horses: in fact, he "crabbed" everything. After the inspection he led the squadron on to a nice piece of grass land where he intended to drill them. He placed himself about 200 yards away, for he had a fine voice and could be plainly heard at that distance. The first order he gave was "Troops, right wheel!" but before the movement was anything like completed, he roared "Halt!" and galloped towards the squadron as hard as he could go, waving the stick which he always carried. "Fall out the officers," he bellowed. When they came to him, he abused them all soundly.

"The drill this morning is shockingly bad: it would disgrace a squadron of yeomanry. You are the most incompetent troop leaders I have ever seen; fall out and let your sergeants lead your troops."

The movement was repeated with the sergeants leading, but the result as far as the major was concerned was the same.

"Fall out the sergeants," he roared. "The senior corporals will lead the troops."

The sergeants were similarly told off and the senior corporals took the lead. The drill was by no means brilliant, but Stephens had now worked off his evil mood and was beginning to be himself again. After a few minutes of this the officers returned to their troops, a few movements were gone through and we went back to billets.

I was too astounded by all that I had seen to know quite what to think of it. Here was Davidson, who had got several years' service, sent off parade for inefficiency, when I knew that he was one of the most brilliant officers in the regiment. I had heard a lot about not telling off officers and N.C.Os. before the men, but here on the first parade that I attended I had seen these rules utterly disregarded. Five minutes after the parade the whole thing was forgotten, and Major Stephens was in the best of tempers. It was only when I asked Duff about the astonishing events of the morning that he explained how an officer must lead a double life: nothing that happens on parade matters in the mess.

"But about telling off the troop leaders and sergeants in front of the men?"

"It doesn't matter a bit what happens at drill. All drills are one continual roar from start to finish; it doesn't matter how much you are abused. It means nothing whatever: it is just part of the ordinary routine, that's all. It is all forgotten five minutes after the parade. You will soon get as used to it as I am."

I have said that this was the first parade I attended. I shall not forget it very easily.

CHAPTER 3

My First Taste of War

On November 15th we moved to new billets at Vaudring-hem, and on December 4th I was sent up with a number of other junior officers in the division to be attached to the infantry in the Loos sector for a fortnight, in order to get some idea of trench warfare before being put in command of men in action. This was a very sound idea, and I was very grateful for the knowledge which I had gained there, when the division went up dismounted after Christmas, for it is obviously not easy for a young officer to command men in trenches when he does not know anything about the conditions of life there.

Prendergast, another of our officers, came with the party, and Stephens went to the Infantry Brigade Headquarters to gain some experience of staff work, for which he had considerable aptitude. In addition to being a first-rate regimental soldier, he had also considerable administrative ability, and was as good at handling papers as he was at handling men.

We entrained at Lumbres at 7 a.m. and about eleven arrived at Béthune, where we had some lunch in the little restaurant opposite the station. At this time Béthune was almost intact. Bombing was unknown, and the only damage which the town had suffered had been caused by a few long-range shells which arrived from time to time.

None of the inhabitants had left the town and life was practically normal, for all the shops appeared to be well stocked, and you could buy almost anything you wanted.

After lunch we were taken in buses to Brigade Headquarters at Mazingarbe, where we were "dished" out to various battalions. Prendergast and I were sent to the 1st Battalion of the Gloucesters, he to "A" Company, and I to "B." We started off with a guide, who took us along the road through Philosophe and Loos and finally landed us at Battalion Headquarters, which were in a ruined house just north of the village. It was a very foggy day and you couldn't see more than forty or fifty yards. We had a lot of guns close to the Philosophe-Loos road, and every now and then I heard a word of command out of the fog, followed by the report of the gun and the peculiar squeaking noise which a shell makes when it is rising.

Between Philosophe and Loos, we passed over the trench which had been the German front line before the battle of September 25th. The ground all round here was strewn with material of all kinds, mostly German. There were greatcoats, ammunition pouches, bits of machine-guns, rifles, torn tunics, buttons, boots, cooking utensils, tins of preserved meat, cigar boxes, dud shells, thousands of rounds of ammunition mostly in machine-gun belts, and almost everything that you can think of.

After seeing the colonel, we went off to our companies. "A" Company was commanded by Durant, who was exceedingly good to me all the time that I was there. He showed me all there was to be seen, and gave me all the instruction that he possibly could. "A" Company was at that time in reserve in a trench which had been made by connecting up a number of old German gun-pits, which had contained a battery of field guns before the battle. There were literally thousands of empty shell cases lying about. I heard that that particular battery had been captured during the advance, just as they were limbering up: the battery commander had left it too late and the whole lot were bagged, horses, guns, personnel, and all.

There were only two officers in the company, since they had lost heavily in the attack, and had not yet made up to strength either in officers or men, so naturally Durant and Parnell had their hands pretty full.

These two appeared to do themselves pretty well in the way of messing. For tea they produced eggs, toast, fresh butter, jam and tinned fruit, which, when you come to think of it, is not bad for trench food. About five o'clock the company paraded to march up to the front line, which was about 1,500 yards away. Everything was very quiet, as, I suppose, was natural on a foggy day; I had not heard a Boche shell, and the only sounds were the dull reports of rifles in the distance and the occasional whistle of a bullet overhead. We did the first 600 yards across the open, and then entered a communication trench which soon led into the front line.

At that time there were no trench boards, riveting frames, or other conveniences which were introduced later; you simply had to plough through the mud as well as you could, and I can vouch for the fact that it was no joke, for I had on a pair of gum-boots, and these were pulled off no less than twice during that short distance. The second time that they came off I could not find them for some time, for by now it was pitch dark. A trench in winter never really dries up except during the frosty weather, and this one was especially bad now, because there had been a fall of snow which was just melting, and the snow and the con-tinual traffic up and down had made it into a sort of morass.

The relief of the company in the line was carried out easily enough, and was in great contrast to some of the chaotic reliefs in which I had the misfortune to participate later on. I must say that this sector was a very easy one for finding your way about, as there were no saps and disused trenches in which to get lost. I shall relate presently how another sector, which we occupied when the division came up a month afterwards, was a regular maze of saps, communication trenches, etc., and how easy it was to lose one's way.

It is difficult to describe one's feelings the first time one goes into the front line. It seemed hard to realise that there, 150 yards away, lurked the Huns about whom one had heard so much and who were the cause of our being there. As soon as it was light, I had a good look at the German position and all the country round. The fog had lifted, and I could see a vast expanse of country on three sides of me. In front one could only see about 200 yards, for just behind the Boche front line was a little rise which hid the ground behind from view. I could, however, see the tops of the buildings beyond the ridge.

Behind me and slightly to the right lay what had once been Loos village. Not a single house had a roof left on it, for it had been under the fire of the guns of both sides during the battle, and even now received daily attention from the Huns. On the northern edge of the village stood the double tower at the pit-head of a large mine. This is a wonderful landmark and can be seen for miles. There it stood apparently unharmed by the terrific bombardments which had demolished every house around, and as if in defiance of the mighty blows which the guns of the two nations had dealt it.

Some days afterwards I went close up to it and saw how it had been struck again and again by direct hits, but still the massive iron framework withstood the shocks. When I saw it some weeks afterwards one of the towers had a big list to port, but still stood firm. Beyond the village and further south, I could see the long rise known as the Vimy Ridge, which was to be the scene of much fierce fighting two years afterwards, while behind me I could make out the tops of the houses of the villages some miles back.

North of us the country was one network of trenches. The soil here is chalky and, naturally any place where the ground had been dug shows up white to the eye. Half-right from where I stood the ground rose gently up to the German lines, which on all that front showed up extraordinarily clearly. This rise is known as Hill 70. Before I saw it, I always pictured it as a steep hill, but in reality, it is the gentlest of slopes, so gentle in fact as to be scarcely noticeable. I could see from my position that the whole ground was thickly strewn with dead of both sides, mostly German, for this had been the scene of some very fierce fighting on September 25th, and again on October 8th when the Germans had made a big counter-attack and been bloodily repulsed.

A thing which strikes anyone looking at the country round there is the large number of slag heaps which can be seen on all sides. Half-left I could make out that known as Fosse 8, which was beginning to stand out black and gaunt against the red sky. There had been a lot of fighting round it, and I believe it had been actually taken by a Company of Highlanders during the battle. The whole appearance of this country is one of utter desolation. I don't know why it is, but most of the battlefields which I saw, and the ground over which I fought later on, seemed to be the most desolate country I have ever come across. It seemed hard to believe that somewhere in the wide expanse of country before me were thousands of men waiting to get at each other's throats, and yet not a single one could be seen.

At about eight o'clock we had breakfast, and a very good meal it was. The eggs and bacon tasted better than ever they had at home, and I must say that our cook was a master of his art. Some people abuse soldier cooks, and say they are no good, but my experience has been exactly the opposite.

During the day I walked round with Durant, who explained everything to me. There is a lot to be learnt about the way to put up sandbags, about riveting, drainage, loopholes, etc., how to manage reliefs and a host of other things.

About ten o'clock the Boches sent over the first shell I had ever heard: it was a shrapnel, and burst about fifty yards behind our trench. A dozen more followed in quick succession in exactly the same place. It seemed odd to me that anyone should fire at the same spot the whole time, because it appears fairly obvious that if there is anyone there when the first two or three shots come, he will not be foolish enough to stay there for a dozen.

Night is the most interesting time; everything is as quiet as death except for the *plop-plop* of the Very Lights. Occasionally you can hear the limbers bringing up the rations—sometimes our own, sometimes the enemy's, according to the direction of the wind—but for the most part absolute quiet reigns, especially during the latter part of the night, when the working parties have finished their tasks, and the ration and ammunition limbers clatter back to billets.

Every night we had patrols out under an officer or N.C.O. Patrolling in no man's land between two trench lines is ticklish work, especially when you are close to the enemy's trench. We used to go up to within a few yards of the Hun line, listen for any suspicious noises, crawl along the wire for a hundred yards or so, and then return to our trench. Sometimes we could distinctly see the Huns working, wiring or repairing their trench; we could make out their ugly little round caps and hear them grunting to each other.

The corporal who was with me the first time I went out was a fine fellow. He had been in France since Mons, and was up to all the tricks of the trade. He knew that I was fresh to the game, and the first time we saw a Boche he pointed him out with the delight of a gillie who has brought you to within shot of a stag.

"There 'e be, sir," he whispered. "See 'is square 'ead and round cap; couldn't I just pick 'im off nicely!"

We could easily have shot him and several others, but our orders were only to listen and afford protection to a wiring party of our own. I went out like this, two or three times during my stay with the Gloucesters, but the first night was the only night on which we saw Boches.

Nearly every day our gunners provided us with an amusing sight. They used to carry out concentrated shoots on some particular portion of Hun trench, and it certainly was worth seeing. It appeared to amuse the men, and well it might, for the trench in question became a mass of flying stones, earth, bits of wood and other things, which were said to be arms and legs. The German artillery, on the other hand, was very quiet except on one occasion when they retaliated on our trench, killing five men of our company and wounding twelve.

These were the first casualties I had ever seen. Amongst the killed was an unfortunate boy of eighteen who had only just come out to France. The working of fate is indeed a curious thing. There were some men who had been through the whole war since 1914 and had never been touched, and here was this poor lad killed the first time he went into the front line. On December 18th we returned to our units near Lumbres, and on January 1st a dismounted party was formed out of the division and sent up to take over the sector of the line between the Hohenzollern and the Vermelles-Hulluch road.

The journey up was uneventful, except that owing to lack of fuel in our billets in Béthune some of my men tore up the floor boards, an event which appeared to upset Stephens somewhat, and on account of which I was put under arrest. The sector of the line which we held was very unwholesome. My bit was just opposite to Hulluch quarries, and I think this was one of the most gruesome spots I remember. There were about half a dozen huge craters connected by a maze of trenches, and anyone can imagine that this was a splendid place for getting hopelessly lost, since it was not easy to distinguish one crater from another. My squadron was very much split up. We had six men here, a dozen there, ten somewhere else, each group in different little posts usually on the edge of these infernal craters, and it was by no means easy to find the way to each post at night.

On one occasion we sprang a mine close to the enemy lines and my troop was ordered to take the crater. This does not mean getting into the crater itself, but holding the near edge of it, for to seize the far edge is only to expose yourself unnecessarily and to court disaster.

During this operation I saw a horrible sight. One of my men, Stansfield, had been half buried by the explosion of a trench-mortar shell, and only his head was protruding above ground. This happened outside our trench and only some fifteen yards from the Boches, who were very quick to spot the poor fellow's predicament. Then the awful thing happened. They started throwing stick-bombs at him. The first one landed some yards away from him, but the second pitched about a foot from his head. There was a delay of about three seconds, a report, and I knew it was all over with the poor fellow.

Several of us rushed to his assistance, but it was too late, and we had to see him perish before our eyes.

I do not intend to describe trench life any further, as much has been written on the subject already, and to give a full description of everything I saw would take a volume in itself, but there are some features about a life in the line which are of general interest.

In the first place it is extraordinary what an effect this life has on the men. If there has been any grousing in billets, it stops automatically at the first sound of a shell. I don't know how their minds work, or what their thoughts are, but I have felt the same thing myself. I used to feel very angry with Stephens, who used to curse me into heaps at all times—and, I admit, quite rightly too—when we were in billets or on the march, but the first time I heard a shell or a bullet I used to lose all feeling of resentment, and think only what a capital leader he was. In the same way he used to stop damning and cursing as soon as we got into action.

I suppose that the reason is that danger brings all men together. There is in action a feeling of *camaraderie* which exists nowhere else. The men bring one tea in their mess tins and do all kinds of things for one which they would never do at any other time.

War is a great leveller of persons, someone once said, but he might have stated that it also unites them.

And so, it went on: day after day, night after night we occupied that line until we knew it pretty well. Every four days we changed over from the front line into support, or reserve, and then back into the front line. The casualties were on the whole heavy, but crater-land is not the most wholesome of places.

My troop was on the extreme left of our division, and strangely enough the officer commanding the troop on my left during our first tour in the front line was the unfortunate fellow who had had his eyebrows shaved off at Sandhurst. Even now they had not grown properly, but it is a matter of no moment to him now, for the poor chap was killed by a shell a few days afterwards.

Stephens looked after the squadron splendidly all the time

we were up, and was as cheery as anything. He was a remarkable man, for he could rag with us and do the most absurd things, such as imitating monkeys, standing on his head, etc. at one moment, and the next curse us into heaps and have us all in the palm of his hand. He was much loved by all the men. No matter how much he cursed and swore, he never put their backs up. The reason was that when you were called all sorts of names you had a sort of sneaking feeling that he was right, and even if you tried to make out to other people that you were not to blame you couldn't persuade yourself against your secret convictions.

Often later on when he found fault with me, I used often to try and "Swing it," but he knew very well when an excuse was valid and when it was not. I can only remember one occasion on which I really "swung it" on him.

At the end of February, we returned to billets. No one was sorry to get a bath, and clean clothes.

CHAPTER 4

I am Given a Troop

When we got back, I found that I had been promoted to command a troop. I do not hesitate to say that I felt considerable pride at this: I was told I was lucky to get one so soon.

The regiment had still a good many of the original men and horses that had come out in 1914. My sergeant, by name Coates, was a very smart man, scrupulously clean, and as brave as a lion. He was good at handling men, and was also a good horse-master. He had seen a great deal of service, and was full of the spirit and tradition of the regiment and the old army. He was one of the N.C.Os. of the old school, who are the backbone of a regiment.

For the benefit of the uninitiated I must explain that a troop is organised into four sections, each commanded by a corporal. To my mind the section leaders are the mainstay of the whole fabric, but more of this anon. The billet occupied by most of my troop was a large farm, which had two big barns. Here all the horses were stabled, with the exception of a few which were kept in outhouses, etc.

This billet was occupied by us during the whole of that winter. I believe the men were quite comfortable. Some slept in a nice little room which had tables, chairs and a fireplace, and was very cosy. For bedding they had made palliasses, and in the cold weather there was a roaring fire all night. I think this billet was as comfortable as any. The remainder of the troop slept in a similar room in a farm about three hundred yards away.

There is a tremendous lot to learn about leading a troop. To look after thirty men and about the same number of horses is no light task. Anyone can learn to look after horses after taking a certain amount of trouble, but to lead men is quite a different matter.

An officer may be an expert at handling army corps on the map, he may be able to win battles on paper, sending a division here and a brigade there—but it does not follow that he is able to handle one single man of that brigade himself or to get any man to do things for him. The general who cannot handle men when he is young will never handle armies when he is older. Unless, therefore, an officer has the gift of commanding men, he is no use. If you can feel that you are their real leader and not a mere figure-head, if you know that they will stick by you in a tight place, and that you can get the best out of them, then you can consider yourself to be fit to command, and not till then.

You may be an excellent horseman, a good sportsman, and a good tactician, but this is not enough. You must have personality. This is a thing which no one can develop; it is a gift in itself. You may have many good qualities, and all these will help to a certain extent; but unless you have the magnetism which will make men follow you, you can never hope to lead them with success. You cannot drive them, therefore you must lead.

There is no one more critical than a soldier. They know that you are the man whom one day they will follow into action, and will size you up accordingly. They will soon know all about you, your strong points and your weaknesses. How they know all this I never hope to discover, but know they do and know everything. If the men think that their officer is a good man, then in their eyes everything that he does is right; if not, then no matter what he does someone will have some fault to find with it.

In the German Army the discipline is founded upon fear of punishment pure and simple, but British discipline rests upon the basis of mutual confidence between officers and men. The right way to treat men is with kindness and absolute firmness.

I might say a great deal more on this subject, but what I have already said puts the matter in a nutshell. One of the most interesting studies in the world is that of human nature. "The proper study of mankind is man," said Terence. It is, and also the most interesting. In a command of thirty men there is room for a close study of the character of every man in the troop. You soon get to know which are the clever ones, and which the stupid, but you can go a great deal deeper than that. If you study them properly you can almost tell what each will do under certain circumstances. You can get to know their whole outlook on life.

Some months after the time of which I write I succeeded by a close study of a man's character in getting him to alter materially his whole outlook on the world and his surroundings. This man had been allowed to get into a morbid and depressed condition. The sole cause of this was neglect on the part of his superiors who had failed absolutely to understand him, or else had taken no interest in him. He had thought that he was no good for anything, that any good work he did was not appreciated, and that no one understood him. With a little trouble he soon became a changed man.

As soon as he saw that what he did was appreciated, he began to take a pride in himself. He was rather sensitive by nature, and no sooner did he realise that his officer knew that he had a peculiar temperament and could not help it, and that he was thoroughly understood, then he began to alter. He was extraordinarily gallant in action, and he now holds the Military Medal and has been promoted to corporal. I believe that I saved this man from his morbid condition simply by studying his character and treating him in the right way.

I said just now that to do any good with men you must have personality. But you must also have tact and common sense. You must make them feel that you think of their wants before your own, and you must be absolutely straight with them. The man who has the personality, the common sense, and the tact will do anything with them, and he is the possessor of that for which millionaires would give half their fortunes.

Some years before the war I believe that there was a widespread idea that to be a successful cavalry officer all that was required was to be smartly dressed, to ride well and to spend money freely. I have tried to show that the truth is far otherwise. In war a man cannot hide his true nature. If he is brave his bravery will show itself; if he is a coward everyone will know it. When shells are falling it does not matter how many horses or motor-cars you possess. The only things that matter are your qualities as a soldier.

Before you are anything like efficient a great deal of technical knowledge is necessary. To start with, there are the horses. You can learn enough about these in a month or two to carry on, but good horse-mastership is a lifelong study and can only be acquired by experience. There are many people who are fine riders, and good men to hounds, but who have no more idea of how to look after a horse than of how to fly. If you do not know how to care for horses, what minor ailments to expect and how to treat them, you cannot teach others to do so.

Unless the men are good horse-masters you will have endless sore backs, kicks, rubs, etc., and will never get the best out of a troop. A cavalryman is no good without his horse; therefore, he must know how to look after it and get the best out of it. Horses out here have got diseases which were unknown to veterinary science before the war, and many new discoveries have been made, as the result of close study of the conditions in which they lived. The horse-mastership in the British Army has always been of a very high order, and is the admiration of our Allies.

In rest billets such as these there were endless opportunities of studying horses, and it would have been criminal not to take advantage of them. One of the best ways of learning is to go round with the farrier sergeant and see all the minor ailments attended to. Then there is the shoeing. I was made to put on a shoe two or three times per week until I could do it quickly and efficiently, and was passed out by the colonel.

There is also the care of arms, equipment and saddlery. This is not learnt in a day. The Hotchkiss rifle, of which every troop has one, is a weapon which needs a lot of attention; it takes some weeks to understand this. A cavalryman carries an appalling quantity of kit and equipment. I shall say something about this later on.

In some ways an officer who has been through the ranks has an advantage over the others. He knows from experience just what a soldier can and cannot do. An officer who has not had this experience can only learn by careful study of the men. Books are a help, but you cannot learn how to soldier from them alone. The only way is to see and do the real thing.

CHAPTER 5

The Art of Command

It is by no means an easy thing to command a troop. I have said that a great many of our men had a lot of service and had been out since the beginning of the war. I could not help having some misgivings at first. There was I, aged twenty, with absolutely no experience except what I had gained during the last few weeks, in command of thirty stalwarts, some with many years' service and South African ribbons, others with less service but with the knowledge gained in fifteen months of war. It is one thing to command thirty recruits who know nothing—you feel you know more than they do—but it is quite another affair to run a troop of veteran soldiers, many of whom had been in the army before I was born.

This feeling is only natural if you are at all human. I am not ashamed to say that it was several months before I attained much self-confidence. One dislikes giving orders when one is not sure of oneself.

Major Stephens understood this perfectly, as indeed he understood all our difficulties. He told me that it would take a long time before I felt myself the real troop leader, and he was right.

Nothing is so distressing as making a big blunder. In the first scheme in which I commanded a troop, we were captured lock, stock and barrel, as also we were in the next. This did not encourage me. Again, you feel very awkward if you rebuke a man for something which you believe to be wrong, and discover that he is in the right all the time.

This also happened to me several times. I had always been taught that when halted on the road a man must take his rifle out of the rifle-bucket, so as to relieve the horse's back of as much pressure as possible. The first time that I saw a man committing this atrocity, as I believed, and ordered him to take his rifle out, I discovered that he was a pack leader. Now any man who leads another horse is allowed to keep his rifle in the bucket to facilitate mounting. This kind of thing makes one feel very uncomfortable.

Strangely enough no blunders that you make seem to surprise the men in the least. I have heard them say: "He'll learn in time," or "He's only just come out here," which seems to indicate that they expect it as a part of the ordinary routine. The mind of the British soldier is really an astonishing thing. You would expect them to adopt a very different attitude, but such is not the case provided they think that you are looking after them. If you look after them, they will look after you. I do not mean to say that an officer should give them all kinds of things—indeed I disbelieve in that practice entirely—but there are many little things you can do to make their lives pleasanter than would be the case if you did nothing for them.

The leading light in a troop is of course the troop sergeant. My own was a capital fellow, whom I liked very much. He knew his job thoroughly, was a strict disciplinarian, and was liked and respected by all the men.

Now the great danger in having a very young officer and a veteran sergeant is that unless the officer is strong-minded and wideawake, he will get into the hands of his sergeant who will try and run the show on his own. I have seen this happen several times; in fact, it happened to me at first. Now the troop leader's point of view is not always the same as that of the troop sergeant. The latter is responsible to his officer for discipline, etc., and the temptation is for him to overstep the mark a little and do too much. If you are not very careful you will find that your orders, though necessarily carried out in the letter, are not always so in the spirit, should the troop sergeant not like the idea.

Here the same difficulty, as I have just mentioned, presents itself. No junior officer likes to dictate to a man with twenty years' service and a breast full of medals. It comes back to the same truth: if you have the personality and the force of character to let your sergeant see that he cannot "run" you, all is well, but once let yourself get into the hands of an old N.C.O. and you are done. I had been told this at Sandhurst, and I now realised the absolute truth of it. It is extraordinarily hard to know at first what can be done and what cannot. I was bamboozled many times during the first few weeks by Sergeant Coates, who said that he had been unable to carry out something I wanted done, when he knew perfectly well that he could have done it.

A lot of people believe in trying to get the whole troop together in one farm, so that the troop sergeant can run the whole thing himself. Personally, I am convinced that this is wrong. There are four corporals in a troop, and what are they for if not to command each his own section? The trouble is that if you get a troop all together your sergeant will run the thing on his own, giving orders direct to each man instead of through the corporals. If this is allowed no officer can expect to have corporals with any initiative or power of command; nor will they take any interest in their sections if they are not allowed to command them.

There is nothing I should dislike more than that the squadron leader should come and give direct orders to my N.C.Os., instead of through me. It is just the same with them, and I do not think that this is sufficiently realised. If there is a weak spot in a troop, it will often be found that it is a corporal who is not doing his job. If you look into the matter you will find that the only reason is that he is not allowed to do it. The next thing that happens is that the troop sergeant brings up the unfortunate man for inefficiency. Had the man been allowed to run his own show, probably he would have done it perfectly well. A great deal of judgment is required in these matters, and a faulty appreciation of a case may lead to great injustice.

To my mind the section leaders are the mainstay of the whole thing. Give each section a separate billet and the corporals will begin to take an intelligent interest in their work, take a pride in themselves, their men and their horses, and in short run a good show. If they cannot run a section under those conditions, they will never command one in the field; but the following is also true: if they are not allowed really to command their sections at all times, they will never run them properly either in billets or in action. I have seen troops run both ways, and I am convinced that the latter is the best. Stephens was particularly keen on this point. I have read a lot in the papers about the advantages of decentralisation. This method can and should be applied to soldiering no less than to anything else.

The routine in winter billets was a simple one. Reveille was at 6.30, when the horses were watered and fed. After this they were taken to exercise and then watered and fed again. Then came breakfast about 8.30, and then "stables" at eleven. "Stables" is the business hour of the day. The troop leader visits each section, sees the horses properly groomed, watered and fed, sees any sick men, etc. During "Stables," too, justice is meted out to any miscreants, any orders brought to the notice of those concerned, and any wants or complaints dealt with.

Occasionally Stephens would come round. His speciality was sanitation and the tidiness and cleanliness of the men's billets. He was madly keen about these points and quite rightly. Sometimes, however, he carried things a trifle far: I have known him go into a towering passion over a boot or blanket out of place. So furious did he get on one or two occasions that I never gave him cause for displeasure on this account again.

In the afternoons sometimes there was a musketry parade, sometimes bayonet exercises, but more often a football match or nothing at all.

At 4.30 we had evening stables, after which the men had tea. This finished the day except for feeding the horses again at eight o'clock.

The officers' mess was in a farm at the bottom of the village. It was a charming spot just on the edge of a stream, and reminded me strongly of my own home. The country round was full of farms, and there was heaps to be got in the way of eggs, butter and milk. Every now and then we used to send to the nearest canteen and buy stores. We ran a canteen for the men, at which they could buy almost anything they wanted at cost price. I think everyone was very happy in these billets.

The football matches were great fun. We used to have inter-troop and inter-squadron matches. The former were the most amusing. Stephens encouraged them and gave a prize to the winners.

Occasionally some absurd things happened, usually connected with trouble with the owner of the field. On one occasion an irate and excited woman rushed on to the field and uprooted all four goal posts and the corner flags. This was so unexpected that no one quite knew what to do. Eventually she was pacified by Sergeant Giles, who knew a bit of French, and the game proceeded. When the old woman eventually allowed the game to go on, she was escorted off the field by a number of men and cheered by the whole squadron and called "*bonne madame*" and a number of other nice things which were probably not understood either by the good lady or the men.

On another occasion a farmer rushed on the field and began a heated argument with a corporal whose horses were knocking down his wall. The speed at which these folk talk when excited is really astonishing. When a farmer complains about anything, the rest of his family usually chip in, and all their voices are blended into one; they love to talk all at the same time.

Sometimes the most ridiculous things occurred. Once a couple of horses broke away from their stables and came on to the field; they trotted about on the ground for about half an hour before they were caught. Eventually they began to gallop, and continued round the field kicking and bucking for about ten minutes. A football match seems to attract all sorts of animals. I have seen cows, pigs, goats, sheep and donkeys, which had been peacefully grazing at the other end of the field, stampede and practically take possession of the ground. Why they run in the direction of the thing which is frightening them I have never discovered.

When the ground began to dry up and the weather became more settled, we began some very strenuous training. This commenced with simple schemes for officers and N.C.Os. under Stephens. He was a remarkably good instructor, and his solutions were based on common sense and solid experience. He was very keen on all the men being well turned out and smartly dressed, since, as he said, cleanliness and discipline go hand in hand. This I realised more and more later on.

The first of these schemes took place on a frosty morning in February. The horses had all been clipped and were full of life. My own horse was particularly so, and for some reason elected to rear and cannon into Stephens just as he was inspecting the parade. The suddenness of this attack drove Stephens' horse backwards into the ranks of the N.C.Os. who were formed up in line, and from here it refused to move despite spur, stick and much abusive language. The major was not usually very good-tempered in the mornings and abused every one soundly until Davidson eventually caught the stubborn creature one with his hunting crop which so startled it that it jumped about ten feet forward. During this performance the N.C.Os. sat absolutely rigid, apparently unconscious of the humour of the situation.

After this bad start we got going, and the scheme began. It was a very simple problem—the reconnaissance of a village. Each troop leader had to ride round it with his N.C.Os., decide how to reconnoitre it, and meet the major at the church. I was just riding round the north side of the village when I saw the major approaching at full gallop. Now when Stephens rode at full gallop it usually meant that he had seen something wrong. When he was about a hundred yards off, he began to wave his stick.

"Where are your field-glasses?" he roared.

"In their case," I answered, thinking this the only thing to say.

"Get them out, then," he bellowed, pulling up alongside of me.

"Very good, sir," I said, fumbling with the strap.

In another second I produced the contents, but instead of field-glasses I found that I was holding a packet of sandwiches and a slice of cake. I fully expected to have my head blown off for this, but the major was so struck by the absurdity of the situation that he actually laughed, though he said that field-glasses were meant to be used and not left behind and lunch carried in their place. Stephens certainly possessed a sense of humour; I believe this to be invaluable when dealing with men. My servant, Neame, was responsible for this. I had to tell him that in future I would carry sandwiches in my wallets and not in my field-glass case.

CHAPTER 6

The Ypres Salient

After a number of these officers and N.C.O. staff rides we began schemes with the men; sometimes we would do a scheme for one troop, sometimes the major took out the whole squadron. Each scheme was followed by a "*pow-wow*," at which various points were discussed and mistakes pointed out.

Now before any parade every officer must inspect his command to ensure that the horses are properly saddled up and that the men's equipment is put on in the correct manner. Horses and men must be scrupulously clean and saddlery and steelwork well polished. It is very hard at first to spot any faults, but after a time you get into the habit of detecting things very quickly. The best way of inspecting a troop is to let them mount, then ride along the line mounted yourself. The practised eye will spot any faults immediately.

On parade, before one of our staff rides, Stephens once detected a corporal without a curb-chain. He pointed at the horse's bit with his stick and was about to administer a sound rebuff, but this was never delivered for the horse took fright and before Stephens had got a word out was two hundred yards away round a bend in the road. Where horses are concerned there is an excellent chance of something ludicrous happening.

The secret of success in any scheme, or, for that matter, in the real thing, is to be able to read your map with absolute certainty. The officer or N.C.O. who cannot do this will sooner or later "let himself in" very badly. I can recall examples of mistakes

44

in map-reading which led a body of men to go into a village which was held by the enemy instead of into the one to which they should have gone, and the result was very heavy casualties. Now map-reading is not learnt in a day, and is only acquired by constant practice. It is just as important for N.C.Os. as it is for officers, for they, too, are often detached, with their commands, on some special mission.

As the training advanced, we took part in regimental and brigade schemes on a training ground near St. Omer. These were watched and criticized by the divisional commander. Sir Philip Chetwode, and often by the corps commander as well.

In the cavalry small units are often sent out on independent missions: for instance, a section, troop, or squadron is often out on its own for many hours or even days. This kind of work naturally calls for greater initiative on the part of junior officers and N.C.Os. than would be the case if the units were always with the regiment. Being out on one's own is the pleasantest sensation I know. You have your own show absolutely; there is no one to tell you what to do and what not to do, and it simply depends on yourself whether you are successful or not. Besides this, it is the finest training in the world for anyone to have to depend on his own wits.

Tactical work is really extraordinarily interesting. To begin with, it cannot be studied as an exact science. I say "science," for it certainly is a science. There are certain broad principles which everyone must follow. To break these is to court disaster; but the detail can only be learnt by experience. Personally, I believe that one of the best ways of learning anything is to watch other people who are experts, and to try to imitate them. A good deal of knowledge can be acquired in this way, but the most profitable learning is that which is derived from a man's own mistakes. No one profits much by other people's.

I said just now that there are certain broad principles on which everyone must go. This is absolutely true; at the same time some of the most brilliant victories have been won by disregarding these principles. To depart from these rules, however, is not for beginners: at school, when learning Latin verses, a boy may not end a pentameter line with anything except a two-syllabled word; in music an elementary contrapuntist may not write consecutive fifths; both these rules, however, may be disregarded on becoming more advanced. It is just the same with soldiering: to take liberties is to assume the privileges of an expert.

Sir Philip Chetwode was a remarkably good instructor. He always had a *pow-wow* at the end of each scheme, and gave remarkably lucid explanations of the reasons why this or that was wrong. He advocated the working out of simple schemes when out for walks, or when lying awake in bed. This may seem absurd, but it is sound enough. No one can consider himself efficient unless he has trained himself to prepare for any eventuality. There are hundreds of different situations which may stare an officer in the face at any time: if he has not foreseen the possibility of these, he will not be able to deal with them. I always remembered this saying of General Chetwode; and on several occasions, two years later, I profited materially by having followed his advice.

Those days in the unspoiled country behind the lines were some of the pleasantest I can recall. The village where we were billeted was a delightful spot and the country all round was charming. From our mess we looked across a valley with thick woods on the other side; along the bottom ran a stream where there was an abundance of trout, and just at the corner of a copse on the river banks was a mill. Near this mill were several shady pools, which were favourite haunts of mine during the fishing season. Here one could spend an hour and forget the war altogether. Along the road which crossed the river at this point I used to see the cattle come shambling along every evening; the farmer's daughters used to pass along with their foaming milk-pails, and at certain hours the children would pass by on their way to and from school. It seemed incredible that twenty miles away there raged the most terrific conflict that the world has ever seen.

We remained in that village until June 2nd. On this day the Germans delivered a heavy attack on the Canadians in the Ypres

Salient. Hooge was taken, and the Germans reached the outskirts of Zillebeke and penetrated close to Ypres itself.

I believe the cavalry were at that time practically the only reserves which we possessed. The authorities decided to bring us up, and that evening we "*embused*" for the threatened point, in case the enemy should attempt to exploit his initial success. It would have been useless to send us up mounted, for what could horsemen do in that country, which is nothing but shell holes and barbed wire?

There is something sinister about a fleet of buses. The sight of a column of these grey monsters somehow reminds one of trenches and trench warfare.

It is some two hours' run from Lumbres to Ypres; the roads were good and in those days were not encumbered by the heavy traffic which passed along them later on. It was dark when we reached Poperinghe; when we were clear of the town, we could see the Very Lights distinctly, and knew that we were nearing our destination. Here there was a long wait: apparently it had not been decided where we were going to. After about an hour we went on to Reninghelst, a village some four miles south of Ypres, and were put into huts for the night. Here we remained for two days. On June 5th we marched up past the Café Belge near Dickebusch to Château Ségard, which lay just on the western outskirts of Voormezeele. We occupied a reserve trench and made up a scheme of defence.

This *château* must have been a lovely spot in peace time. Now it was smashed almost beyond recognition. A great shell had landed in the drawing-room, making havoc of all the furniture and pictures. There were the remains of two fine old family portraits, some very handsome chairs and a grand piano, which had been cut almost clean in half by the explosion. The dusty keys were unharmed. I wonder who was the last person who played upon them.

There is something indescribably sad about a ruined home. I could not help thinking of the summer of two years ago when the owner would still have been in occupation, with no thought of the appalling disaster which was to overtake him before the falling of the leaves.

I passed out of the drawing-room through the hall, and into other rooms. Everywhere the destruction was the same. In what must have been the best bedroom a great fourposter was still standing. Bits of charred blankets and bedroom utensils were still lying about covered with dust and cobwebs. A huge hole in the floor marked the spot where a great shell had crashed through into the drawing-room beneath. Another room must have been the nursery, for here were two small iron beds and the remains of some toys. I even found an English Grammar and a "Chardenal." I wonder where the youthful owners of that room are now. I left the house and passed out into the grounds, which extended to several acres.

There was a lawn with a fountain in front of the house, and flower-beds with roses in bloom. There was a greenhouse, now a heap of glass splinters and broken flowerpots, and the remains of a "Ransome" mowing machine. In the kitchen garden there were still rows of vegetables: asparagus, and even strawberries, almost ripe. Most of the garden wall was still standing, though great gaping holes had been rent in it every few yards. The whole place was a terrible picture of desolation. A carriage drive led from the house out into the Ypres-Voormezeele road. In pre-war times it had been fringed with a well-kept lawn: now the grass was a foot or more long and was in some places fit for hay.

From the entrance gate the ground eastwards was flat for about 500 yards; after that it began to slope gradually upwards towards the top of the ridge where the German lines were. The German front line was some 200 yards on our side of the top of the ridge, and about 1,500 yards from the *château*. Amongst the trees just behind the German position was Hollebeke Château, just visible from where I stood. I now saw what an immense advantage the enemy had over us on the ridge; however, the horrors of the Ypres Salient have been described by others! I will not attempt to do so here.

In case we should be required in the front line the officers reconnoitred the route up to a certain point. It is an interesting walk from Château Ségard past Bedford Lodge and on towards Zillebeke. I was struck by the death-like silence of the place. At this time, I reconnoitred the way there was scarcely a sound. Occasionally an odd shell would sail over, apparently meant for one of our batteries, but that afternoon the silence of death reigned over the place.

That evening our guns began a bombardment of the German position, and this, added to the noise of the German artillery, which replied vigorously, made a pretty considerable din. Our trench, which ran through the kitchen garden, received a little attention, as also did the road at the end of the grounds; but the casualties numbered very few.

After three days it became evident that we should not be required and we were "lorried" back to billets. The march back to Reninghelst was not pleasant: heavy rain had fallen for two days and the ground was one huge morass. Every few yards someone fell down, and Sergeant Coates pitched head first into a shell-hole full of water. He was a fine sight when he came out. Marching across country in the dark is no easy matter.

When we reached billets, we found that the division was to move to the Hazebrouck area the next day. The march was not a long one. All our horses were in the open and the weather was ideal all the time that we were there. Our regiment was for a few days at Rue de Bois and then at Pradelles.

At this time our training consisted as much of practice at dismounted work as it did for mounted work. We had to be experts at both. Accordingly, in August, two officers of each regiment were sent up into the line to become acquainted with the latest trench "dodges." I was one of those selected from our regiment and was first sent to the Australians, some of whom were in the "Plugstreet" Sector. Here I had an interesting time. I learnt a number of the latest "wheezes," saw the latest model of dug-out, and realised that a number of novelties and improvements had come out since our last tour in the line.

"Plugstreet" is a very ordinary-looking place. To reach the

front line you walk along a duck-board track right through the wood, and just before reaching the edge you enter a communication trench. The German lines were about sixty yards from our trench. This was the only time I ever came in contact with the Australians. They seem absolutely different from our men. They are mostly men who have "run their own show" at home; most of them, I was told, had their own farms. Consequently, they are far more self-reliant than men who have always been under an employer, or who have not been used to a life of independence. An Australian seems a totally different being to a British soldier.

After three days I was sent to another sector on the Messines Ridge, close to the St. Eloi craters. This was an extraordinarily interesting spot, but not attractive. Sanctuary Wood, Hill 60, and other places round there are not such as to make a suitable holiday resort. I often wondered how many men had been killed within a radius of three miles of where I was. While I was there the German artillery was, on the whole, quiet. The trench-mortars were, however, very troublesome, and caused many casualties. The arrival of these was more frequent than at Vermelles, and those which the Huns now employed seemed to be of a greater degree of frightfulness than those which he had been in the habit of using a few months before.

The most eerie time in this part of the line was at night. You seemed to see star-shells in front, on both sides of and behind you. You got the impression that you were almost completely surrounded.

Men have told me that they would sooner have taken part in a battle such as was then raging on the Somme than sit for weeks in a spot like this. I had, as yet, had no taste of open warfare, but later on I became of the same opinion.

Here I went down one of the great mines which had been bored under the German positions. It is a curious feeling, going down one of these. We started by climbing down an iron ladder a hundred feet sheer. At the bottom of this descent the gallery commenced to run towards the German lines. For the first hundred yards you could walk upright; for the next you had to bend, for the third you had to go on hands and knees, and the last bit had to be done by crawling. The greatest silence was necessary here; the point we had reached was underneath the German reserve trench, and here the mine chamber was being prepared, and explosives heaped up by men stripped to the waist, and working without a sound.

By means of a special instrument we could hear the Boches working in their trench above us. It was odd to know that a few yards away was a trench full of Huns unaware of the fate that was one day to overtake their trench and its occupants. Ventilation was managed by a pump at the mouth of the shaft. It was three hours before I reached daylight again.

This mine was, I believe, one of those which blasted the way to the capture of the Messines Ridge the following June.

After three days in this sector I was sent on to Ypres. Here I lived under the ramparts near the Menin Gate, and visited the Railway wood sector at night. This is not quite such a ghastly spot as the country south of the Menin Road. I do not know why, but the place I had just come from seemed to be far more horrible. However, German artillery seemed to be more active here; every now and then during the night, shoots would be carried out on various cross-roads which traffic had to pass. Dusk was the favourite time for these shoots, for everyone knew that this was the hour when rations and working parties began to come up.

The traffic along the main road was at times something co-lossal, and the noise inseparable from a column of limbers on a *pavé* road was such that Fritz must have heard them. As a matter of fact, you can hear enemy traffic plainly when the wind is the right way. In addition to the limbers there were often columns of troops relieving or relieved, ration parties, working parties, carrying all manner of material, telephone operators laying wires, etc., etc.

After six days here I met my horse outside Ypres and rode back to billets *via* Dickebusch, Locre and Bailleul.

CHAPTER 7

On the Somme

When I got back, I found that Stephens had begun a "horse-strafe." By this I do not mean strafing the horses, but, on the other hand, strafing the officers who were not good horse-masters. As it happened, about this time I had a regular epidemic of kicks, bites, sore backs and lameness in my troop. No matter how careful you are, every troop seems to have spells like this occasionally.

It was unfortunate that I was the victim of this epidemic just when the horse-strafe started, since it meant that Stephens visited me every day and looked at everything in turn. I forget how many times I was put under arrest, and how many of the men he threatened to send to the infantry, but in the end the strafe passed on to another troop.

No one is ever the worse for a "strafe," or "hate," no matter what it is about. During my time out here, I have been the victim of many. It does not matter whether you are really at fault or not: it does everybody good to be "bitten" occasionally. At one moment it would be horses, at another saddlery, at other times emergency rations, proper fitting of clothing, or gas-masks. Strafes came round in cycles.

A peculiar thing I noticed is this: sometimes a certain wheeze suddenly becomes the vogue, whether it be in horse-mastership, tactics, turn-out, or anything else. It continues to be the thing to do for several months or even years, and everyone is led to believe in it. Then comes a change. It suddenly becomes the one thing you must not do. There is something delightfully comical about this. Orders come round to say that any disregard of this principle will give cause for disciplinary action, etc. You begin to wonder how you were ever allowed to do it before.

The commonest of the strafes was that of horses and horse-mastership; on most occasions they were fully justified. A kick or a sore back can usually be avoided, and it is, as a rule, the result of bad supervision. If a troop leader does his job and trains his section leaders to do theirs, there will be very little trouble of this kind. The men are on the whole good horse-masters and require little teaching; on the other hand, supervision is absolutely indispensable. A troop leader is there to supervise, and this is his chief duty.

It is just the same with the men's dress. It makes all the difference in the world if a man's clothes fit or not, or are well or badly put on. This is especially the case with *puttees* and spurs. If the men see that their officer takes a pride in their appearance, they will keep themselves smart where conditions allow. Personally, there is nothing I dislike more than seeing a man with dirty buttons and boots, and spurs and *puttees* badly put on. It is only a question of spending a few minutes more in dressing, and it makes all the difference in the world.

At the end of August, we heard that we were going south for training. We were told to see that all the men's marching order was complete. Kit and necessaries were issued with a liberality which I had not seen before; we were also ordered to sharpen swords and bayonets.

As soon as this last order was given out everyone knew that we were not going training: we thought it far more probable that we were going down to the Somme where our offensive had been progressing well. On September 8th we left billets and began the march southwards. The first march was a short one, only about fourteen miles. Luckily it was fine; the horses were picketed out in a field and cover easily found for the men.

It is very interesting to march through fresh country. Staying long in billets never does a regiment any good: things are bound to get somewhat slack. For some reason the men are always happier when on the move. If there has been any grousing in billets, it always stops immediately one gets on the march. This applies to all ranks from general down to private.

When a regiment moves, a billeting party is always sent ahead to arrange quarters for the night, so that the incoming troops may not be kept waiting about. There is nothing more annoying than to have to hang about waiting to go into billets. A representative of each troop is usually sent; in this way everyone can be shown where to go immediately on arrival.

The march was continued on September 9th to Bours, a nice little village just clear of the coal country. On the way we passed through country of all kinds, industrial and agricultural. Near Camblain were some kind of R.A.F. Headquarters, and here curiously enough I saw Black, my old instructor at Sandhurst, standing by the roadside.

At Bours the squadron was billeted in a stubble field; nearly every one slept outside, including most of the officers, who slept in the orchard. During the night Walton suddenly became aware that a cow was sniffing at him and licking his face. This caused him to wake up with an oath and throw anything he could catch hold of at the brute, which galloped off in hot haste. In the morning we found that the nocturnal visitor had chewed his cap almost to shreds. Walton did not appear to see as much humour in the affair as we did.

Next day we marched to Haut-Maisnil, *via* Valhuon, Conteville, Linzeux and Fillièvres. We arrived in good time, and in the evening, I walked with Stephens to Bachimont. The country just here is extraordinarily pretty. Most of this part of France is nothing but flat arable land and gently rolling hills; but Bachimont stands on the outskirts of a large wood on the top of a fairly steep slope. Beneath it lay miles of cornfields and clover. Most of the corn had been cut, but had not yet been carried in. The whole valley beneath was a vast expanse of corn-stooks, and the setting sun on these made a fine picture.

Next day we moved on to Outrebois. On the way we took part in a brigade scheme. It was not particularly interesting and was only remarkable for the speed at which Hunt, who was second in command of the regiment, led our squadron which formed the regimental reserve. We galloped through scores of root fields, over hedges and ditches and up and down steep banks almost all day. Personally, I was anxious to spare our horses as much as possible, since we were nearing our destination, and I had no wish to have them exhausted before we started the attack.

On the 12th we went on to Havernas. Here the horses of the whole regiment were in one field. There was not much room. I slept on some straw in a cart and was very comfortable.

One of the greatest marvels of our organisation was the supply of forage and rations when a division was on the move. Each day railhead had to be in a different place, which must be previously arranged. From railhead motor-lorries conveyed the supplies to the Brigade Supply dumps, whence they were drawn by the horse transport of each regiment. There was plenty of room for mistakes in an organisation of this kind, but I scarcely ever remember not getting our stuff where there was a decent railway line.

A cavalry brigade on the march was an imposing sight. The column seemed to be unending and was, in fact, something like three miles in length. Besides the three regiments there was a machine-gun squadron, a battery of Royal Horse Artillery, a Field Ambulance and a Veterinary Section. It seemed big enough on the road, but bigger still when it had to be billeted and fed.

The following day we went on to La Neuville, a village on the Ancre, just outside Corbie. Here we arrived about 6 p.m. The whole division was bivouacked along the river bank; there were horses as far as one could see. The next afternoon we rode up to Bray. As we came on to the big ridge along which runs the Corbie-Bray road we could see Albert and, farther on, portions of the shattered woods near Mesnil and Ovillers-la-Boisselle, where we saw occasional shrapnel bursts. Here the thing that caught the eye was the astonishing number of sausage balloons. I counted no less than twenty-six.

We bivouacked in the valley just north-west of Bray village.

As soon as the horses had been groomed, watered and fed, the officers of the brigade were assembled by Sir Philip Chetwode, who explained that a big attack had been arranged for the next day and that five British and Indian Cavalry Divisions and several French Divisions were to take part. He gave no details, saying that the brigadiers and C.O.'s would do that; but he urged us to apply the lessons learned during our long training, and not to forget the three C's of soldiering, "Cheerfulness, Courage and Cunning."

After this our brigadier addressed us.

Gentlemen, the battle in which you will take part tomorrow, if successful, will have far-reaching results. During the past weeks you have been trained in every duty which it can fall to your lot to carry out: it is now up to you to apply the principles which you have learnt. Everyone will, I know, do his best. Be bold, but do not barge into brick walls. Whatever happens, bad or good, I am responsible and I have the greatest confidence in you; I wish you the best of luck.

That evening the colonel explained the scheme to the squadron leaders, and they in turn to us.

I cannot recall all the scheme, but I remember that the infantry were to attack Flers, Guillemont and Ginchy as a first objective. I believe that the second objective was the line La Barque, Gueudecourt, Les Boeufs, Morval.

As soon as the infantry had got these objectives, cavalry was to pass through and seize the high ground on which Bapaume stands. French cavalry was on our right and were to push on in the direction of Sailly-Saillisel and Manancourt.

The attack was to begin at 6 a.m. The whole of that night there was a terrific bombardment and the sky was lit up along the whole horizon; the cavalry was to be ready to move at half an hour's notice. About eight o'clock we heard that our infantry had reached their first objectives, and the order was given to saddle up. I expected the order to mount at any time, but this did not come. Later we heard that the infantry were held up short of the second objective, and we off-saddled again. We saddled up again later on, but to no purpose.

Now the secret of success in a cavalry operation of this kind is that it should be a surprise. When we did not take part the first day, I feared that we should not bring it off at all. The Boches were able to bring up reserves by rail in twenty-four hours. From this moment I think most people despaired of a cavalry success of any magnitude. We had patrols out working with the infantry, but even these were soon withdrawn, since a reconnaissance ascertained that there was another strongly wired line in front of Le Transloy and Bapaume. The whole thing was terribly disappointing. There were dozens of officers who had never as yet taken part in a cavalry operation, and were itching to do so.

We stayed in that bivouac some days, and then moved to another camp on the hill between Dernancourt and Morlancourt. Here the whole division remained until November 8th. Meanwhile bad weather set in, and the bivouac became a morass with mud a foot deep. We could hardly find the horses in the morning, to such an extent were they covered with mud.

I think this was the most depressing time of the war: we had only two tents per troop, and the men were very uncomfortable. The officers "scrounged" some timber from the XIV. Corps and built a hut for the mess and a recreation room for the men, but ours was a draughty, cold place. A dug-out would have been better.

During this time, we sent innumerable working parties up to the line. As each village was captured, we cleared it of debris and corpses: we laid innumerable telegraph and telephone wires, and dug any quantity of trenches. The slaughter at Gueudecourt had been terrific. There was a sunken lane between it and Les Boeufs which was literally heaped with dead, both British and German.

I think that this kind of work depresses the men more than anything. They had all been trained up to the pitch for a cavalry operation, and here we were ploughing through mud, making roads and burying corpses. They had pictured themselves gal-

THE BIVOUAC BECAME A MORASS WITH MUD A FOOT DEEP.

loping over open country with the land of trenches and wire behind them, but now we were faced with the grim reality: it was no cavalryman's war. Under these conditions it was no easy task to keep up the men's spirits: dull times in billets can be relieved by various amusements, but what could we do under these conditions?

Occasional reconnaissances were sent out to get officers acquainted with the country. I went up to Delville Wood and saw Bapaume, and made out the various villages from the map: from a rise just north of Ginchy one could see for miles. I could make out the points which had been the cavalry objectives on September 15th, and could see the Le Transloy line which was now holding us up.

On October 15th I was sent up to a divisional ammunition column near Carnoy with thirty pack-horses in order to help carry up ammunition to the batteries in action. The roads and tracks were now so muddy that limbers could hardly get along.

Every other night I went with my thirty pack-horses, and a lot of mules as well, up to Guillemont station where we drew ammunition and carried it to the various batteries.

Usually we had to wait several hours at Guillemont station. The time of arrival of the train was never known, and there were always several hundred pack animals and limbers waiting to load up from it. The "Guillemont Express," as we called it, usually arrived in two halves. Sometimes I was ordered to draw H.E., sometimes shrapnel shell, sometimes both. I was seldom able to fill up from the first half. It was only a light railway and did not carry much. The result was that I never got away with my load until one or two in the morning. From here I had to go sometimes to a battery at Les Boeufs, sometimes to Morval, sometimes only to Ginchy.

Now bringing a column of animals along roads crowded with traffic going in each direction is no easy matter, especially in the pitch dark. To make matters worse more than half the journeys I did were done in the rain. It is the easiest thing in the world under conditions like these to lose both your com-

(2) ROUGH MAP ABOUT 4 MILES TO 1 INCH

mand and the way as well. At a cross-road traffic control N.C.Os. have an exasperating habit of letting a portion of your command come past and then stopping the remainder to give a party coming from one of the side roads a chance. This happened to me several times.

On one occasion I looked round and saw myself followed by six of my party instead of seventy-five. I went back to the cross-road and, pushing my way through the crowd, I saw the remainder going down the wrong road. You can imagine my feelings at that moment. Before I reached the head of them and got them back on the right road half an hour had gone by, and I even had some trouble to find the faithful six I had left. Just as we got moving again the Huns opened a "shoot" on the cross-roads. Our tail was not yet clear, and three men and several horses were hit, one of the men being killed. To get the party away from the danger spot, and the wounded removed in the pitch dark, was not easy owing to the dense traffic. That night I was only going to one of the Ginchy batteries, quite a short journey, but still it was daylight before I had got the shells unloaded and brought my command back to Carnoy.

The Somme battlefield was the best place I knew for getting lost, absolutely and hopelessly. If you get lost in an inhabited district you can always ask the way, but here the terrific bombardments had so levelled everything that might have served as a landmark that once lost it was practically impossible to get your bearings except by the stars. Usually, as I have said, the nights were dark and overcast if not rainy.

On one occasion I had been to a battery near Les Boeufs. I had a guide who took us there and, on the way back had put us on to a track leading on to the Ginchy road, which he said was only 500 yards away. I then allowed him to go back to his battery. After going a good deal more than this distance and not striking the road, I began to have a fearful feeling that we were lost. Instead of the road, I saw before me a trench and a line of barbed wire. I followed this to the right for a little but could not get through: the trench bent back to the left here and then to the right again; there seemed to be trenches everywhere.

The situation was awkward, for there was only an hour of darkness before us and, in our present position, we should have been in full view of the German lines. This occasion is one of the only ones on which I used my compass. I took the party back a short distance and then started off going almost due south-west, in which direction Ginchy lies from Les Boeufs. This direction incidentally was practically at right angles to the one in which we had been going. After half a mile we struck the road.

It is all very well getting lost when you are alone, but when you have seventy-five men and a hundred and fifty horses and mules behind you it is not pleasant. No one who has not experienced the feeling can know what it is like.

It is a strange thing that no soldier ever knows the way to any place about which you may ask. Officers do occasionally, but men—never. After all, why should they? They have no maps. Every man ought, however, to know the name of the place where he is; but, although it may sound incredible, I am perfectly sure that fifty *per cent.* of a body of men in a village, where they may have been anything up to two or three days, do not know the name of it. Not a single man, except the N.C.Os., will know the names of the villages on either side and in front of him.

Guides are most unreliable people; but it is not so easy to find the way to a place in the dark, even if you have been there in the day. It is harder still to retrace your steps. Anyone who knows the desolation of the Somme will bear witness to this fact.

I reconnoitred the way to all our batteries in the day-time. Map references are very little use. In that country, unless you have been to the actual spot, it is practically impossible to find the place in the dark.

During the first few days of November I returned to the regiment at Dernancourt. I was not sorry to have the artillery mules, with which I had been charged, taken off my hands. A mule is an extraordinary creature: one wet day when I took them down to water, those on one side of the trough with their faces to the wind and rain would not drink until they had been taken to the other side. On another occasion I saw one charge a tent with such force that he uprooted most of the pegs and tore the canvas to ribbons.

Although life on Mount Misery, as we called it, was pretty wretched, there were one or two occurrences which were not entirely devoid of humour. On one occasion a rat invaded the tent in which some of us slept. Ingham, who had a particular aversion to these animals, woke up at 2 a.m. to find the brute running about on his face and amongst his blankets. The next moment the whole tent was in an uproar. Ingham's oaths were accompanied by the indiscriminate hurling of boots in all directions. The rat escaped, but Walton—who had been the victim of a cow at Bours—received one of Ingham's boots on his head, which almost led to a difference between these two then and there.

On another occasion a horse which had got loose in the night actually came and calmly grazed inside the tent. When frightened away it became entangled in the tent ropes and almost brought the canvas down on the top of us.

On November 8th the division left for billets near Hesdin. It took three weeks or more before the saddlery and men's equipment was fit to be seen again.

CHAPTER 8

The Cavalryman and His Equipment

There was a remarkable difference in men's spirits when going up to the line and coming back from it. If they felt they had really achieved something before coming away, well and good, but if not, they never seemed very happy at the prospect of a prolonged stay in billets.

Coming back to rest was one thing in the infantry, but quite another in the cavalry. The infantryman had only himself and his equipment to look after: when he came into billets, he was very soon able to "get down to it," and the time out of the line was a real rest for him. I believe that he had a deal of training to carry out, but at any rate he had the afternoons free.

It was very different in the cavalry. Practically every man had two horses to look after. On paper a troop might have a man to almost every horse, but allowing for cooks, saddlers, and shoeing smiths who could seldom, if ever, look after their horses, you very soon came down to one man to every two horses. You had also to count sergeants and men on leave. When leave was going well, the proportion was even worse than this. To look after three horses, saddlery, his own arms and equipment, to do occasional fatigues, was a full day's work for any man. There was also a guard of a corporal and three men over the horses at night: one of these was on duty at a time. A man would have to do a guard every three or four nights.

I propose here to say something about the cavalryman's equipment and arms. A cavalryman with all his saddlery, gear, arms, ammunition, etc., puts a weight of something like seventeen to eighteen stone on a horse. This may sound ludicrous, but it is true nevertheless. Of course, it is far too heavy, but how is it to be lightened? It is astonishing how much is required to equip a man and a horse for war. I know that brigadiers and commanding officers have made many suggestions for lightening and improving our marching order; but the most valuable are those which come from the man who actually carries the stuff. I have heard several very practical suggestions from the men.

In the first place the most clumsy thing which is carried is the cloak. Rolled on the back of the saddle it is a fearful lump; besides this it makes the saddle top-heavy.

Now some kind of warm coat is certainly necessary. But why not give us a strong thick trench coat, something after the pattern of a Thresher? This will roll up to half the size, and be just as warm.

Another suggestion is to have a light rainproof coat and a detachable woollen lining. The coat would be very convenient rolled on the back and the fleece lining would easily go on the front of the saddle.

Another great drawback to a cloak is the weight of it when wet. I have seen one wet through and plastered with mud weighing over 100 lbs. An objection to the waterproof coats I have suggested might be the expense, but surely the difference could not be so very great?

I believe that considerable improvement is possible in the remainder of the men's equipment. A cavalryman loaded with haversack, water-bottle, ammunition, box respirator, wire cutters, etc., as they are carried at present, is an uncomfortable looking individual. In 1916 I saw an experimental webbing equipment of such a pattern that all the above could have been carried with far more convenience and comfort. I have not discovered why it was never issued.

I now come to a subject in which I beg to differ from my superiors, and that is the matter of Hotchkiss guns and packs. Every troop has a Hotchkiss gun carried on a pack, a tool pack consisting of picks, shovels and sundry other articles, a pack carrying ammunition either for the Hotchkiss gun or for rifles, and every other troop also in 1916 had a ration pack. There was also in the regiment an explosive pack, a stationery pack, and one carrying extra signalling equipment. The last three did not matter much as there was only one of each in the regiment.

The great drawback to a number of these packs is that you feel that your mobility is decreasing. It is a pleasant feeling to feel that you have thirty men behind you, each with his own horse, and unencumbered by packs. But when you know that you have no less than four of the latter in your troop you feel that they will be in trouble at the first obstacle. This feeling is usually justified, for I shall recount later how my packs managed to get into every ditch, bog, stream, or trench that we encountered.

Another point to consider is that each man leading a pack is one man less to fight.

Now I am well aware that the Hotchkiss Rifle was given to us primarily to increase our fire power. This weapon, we were told, is of the same value as twenty-five men. But is it? From my experience I do not believe it is. I have seen the Hotchkiss in action at Cambrai, Amiens and on many other occasions, but I do not consider that they were worth the trouble expended on them. I would sooner have had another six men in my troop if it had been possible.

A Hotchkiss cannot keep up the sustained fire of a Vickers: you cannot keep firing for hours. But the great drawback is that it is appallingly hard to keep them working in muddy weather. After the Battle of Amiens in March, 1918, nearly all our Hotchkiss were out of action for one reason or another, while the machine guns were not.

They may save men, and the man power question has been acute; but I do not believe that a troop is any more efficient with this weapon than without.

A tool pack and an ammunition pack are most useful and necessary, but I think we could do without the others.

CHAPTER 9

The Battle of Arras

About this time Gen. W. H. Greenly, C.M.G., D.S.O., was appointed to the command of our division, Sir Philip Chetwode having gone to Egypt.

General Greenly was a man with an extraordinary insight into people's characters. He possessed also a remarkable faculty for remembering names and faces, even when he had only seen them once. This trait of his character made him extremely popular with all ranks, especially with the junior officers and the rank and file. He possessed also a peculiar capacity for detail. Everything he undertook was carefully worked out beforehand. He was one of the most thorough men I have ever known. He appeared to understand the point of view of the subalterns and private soldiers, and was always willing to give any help he could. At the same time, he used to "chase" the slack and inefficient unmercifully.

One day he inspected my troop billets. I am not shy of saying that it was a really good show: all the men's equipment was spotlessly clean and everything well arranged. At an inspection of this kind "swank" is the thing. It makes all the difference if your cook has a white apron on and brightly polished boots and spurs, and if the sanitary man has painted the regimental colours on the latrine. I was pleased to see that General Greenly spoke to each corporal in turn. I wondered whether he held the same views as I did about the individuality of section leaders.

These inspections are really great fun if you take them in

the right way; at any rate they provided me with considerable amusement. A divisional commander with his staff makes an imposing array at any time, and at this inspection he arrived in all his glory. The inspection was timed for 12 noon. At that hour two large cars arrived outside my farm containing General Greenly, his G.S.O.I., the A.A. and Q.M.G., and another officer on the divisional staff. Waiting at the gate of the farm were our brigadier, the brigade major, and the staff-captain, besides the colonel, the second in command, the adjutant, and the regimental sergeant-major.

Stephens was, of course, there with Walton, who was second in command of the squadron, and the squadron sergeant-major. The regimental sergeant-major was the picture of smartness, you could have used his boots as a mirror without difficulty. Our squadron sergeant-major looked more ferocious than ever, and his moustache bristled as it only bristled on special occasions.

Stephens had made a searching inspection of the billets himself and had expressed himself well satisfied. The only thing which worried him was that the cook had left his comb on the mantelpiece. At this Stephens flew into such a passion that I thought he was going to hit Dawkins, the unfortunate cook. However, the men were just as much accustomed to Stephens' sudden fits of rage as I was.

When the general was ready, we marched off in half-sections, the general and I in front. The whole company looked like a troop on a route march.

"How are you off?" asked the general.

"Very well, sir."

"Do the men like these billets?"

"They say they are very comfortable. Some of the stables are not up to much though."

"What is the name of this corporal?" he asked as we entered the first section billet.

"Nixon, sir."

"Well, Corporal Nixon, is this where you sleep?"

"Yes, sir."

"Comfortable?"

"Yes, sir."

"Your equipment looks very nice."

"Yes, sir."

It certainly did, for everything was beautifully clean and systematically hung up. The men were delighted at being praised for this. It had taken many days to clean it, and there would have been great disappointment if he had not noticed it. This is where General Greenly was so much appreciated. He knew how many hours' work it had taken to prepare for his visit.

He visited each section in turn and asked each section leader some question about his men, horses or billets. They answered fairly intelligently, although I could see that they were partially dumbfounded by this gorgeous array of generals, staff officers and colonels.

The general had a talk with Dawkins, the cook, who was smarter than he had ever been before, or ever will be again. I had borrowed a white apron for him, and he also had on beautifully polished boots and spurs. This unfortunate man had scarcely recovered from the shock of Stephens' visit, and the appearance of this procession so put the wind up him that he couldn't get a word out to answer any of the general's questions. He could only stand still and stare in blank amazement, holding a huge knife in one hand and dixie in the other.

"How about baths?" asked the general.

Now baths and washing was a thing about which Stephens was particularly keen, and I saw him give me a look, as much as to say: "If you haven't got a bathroom, young man, you'll be 'for it.'"

I had a bathroom, and a fine one, and we all marched there. There is something slightly grotesque about a dozen generals and colonels all looking at a bath. This bath was, as a matter of fact, borrowed for the occasion. It was absolutely useless for it had a hole in the bottom, but nobody except myself, Sergeant Coates, and Belling, my sanitary man, knew it. Belling was superb on this occasion.

"Where do you boil the water?" asked the general.

"In 'ere, sir," said Belling, showing a huge caldron.

"And is this where the men bathe?"

"Yes, sir, in this 'ere bath."

"That looks very nice. So, every man has a bath each week and more often if he wants to?"

"Yes, sir."

Belling was tremendously proud of his bathroom. He also regarded the inspection as a kind of sport. In reality we used tubs, but these did not look so "showy" as the fine porcelain bath. The hole in the bottom had been plastered up with whitewash so as to defy detection.

After this the inspection came to an end. General Greenly never asked ridiculous questions about the number of men on proficiency pay or the next horse to be shod, etc. He was above that kind of thing. He knows that a subaltern has better things to do than to carry a host of figures in his head.

I believe the men see the humour of an inspection like this, too, at least I am quite sure that mine did, except, possibly, the unfortunate cook.

During the winter a divisional school for officers and N.C.Os. was started at Douriezy, a village a few miles from our billets. This was an excellent institution. Apart from getting first-rate tactical instruction, you got to know many officers of other regiments whom one would not have met otherwise.

The commandant of the school was Hunt, normally our second in command. He was a brilliant tactician and had original and up-to-date ideas. He was somewhat feared by the officers who attended the courses, and was in fact reputed to have written over his headquarters:

"All hope abandon ye who enter here."

In January a working party was sent up to Vermelles, but this was so dull as not to be worth telling about. It consisted mostly of laying railway lines and unloading ballast from trucks, a vile occupation for cavalry. However, someone had to do it, so it was no good grousing.

When I came back in March, I found that I was to take over the duties of adjutant instead of Hopkins, who was at the school. This is interesting work. You get an insight into the vast and complicated machinery by which regiments, brigades and divisions are administered. It is quite an education and a change from leading a troop.

In billets there was nothing much to do except office work. I used to go for a ride with the C.O. every morning when there was nothing on.

At the end of March preparations began for a move. No one knew where we were going to, but we guessed it was for another "gap." On April 5th we marched to Hem, near Doullens. This particular day was fine, but for a week there had been nothing but snowstorms. There had been no frost, and the ground was in a fearful state.

On April 7th we went on to Gaudiempre, a village about ten miles from Arras. Here we were told that an attack was to be made on April 9th over the ground between the Vimy Ridge and Henin-sur-Cojeul. If certain objectives were gained by a fixed hour, the 2nd and 3rd Cavalry Divisions were going through to seize a line further east.

The 3rd Division was operating north of the Arras-Cambrai road and ourselves on the south of it. The objective of our division was a line drawn from Fontaine les Croisilles to Vis-en-Artois. The attack was timed for 6 a.m., when the Infantry carried the Vimy Ridge and Telegraph Hill, and everywhere made considerable progress.

We were not brought up until 1 p.m., when we marched *via* Wailly and Arras and formed up on the western slopes of Telegraph Hill. It was a vile day and as cold as could be. There were occasional snowstorms, and the wind was like ice.

As we emerged from Arras on to the flat piece of ground between the town and Telegraph Hill, we passed General Greenly and his staff standing by the roadside with a lance and pennon stuck in the ground to represent Divisional Headquarters. He wished all the officers good luck, and I really thought we were going to achieve something.

But we were not taken any farther than Telegraph Hill. The infantry objectives had not been gained and it would have been criminal to launch ten thousand cavalry against a trench line defended by wire.

The country in front of us was very open and consisted of gently-rolling hills. It was not, however, as flat as the Somme.

Patrols went forward to keep touch with the infantry, but that was all that we did that day.

The ground where we had been assembled came in for a little shelling, but there was very little damage. Had the Hun known what lay behind that slope, they would have shelled the place more heavily, for a division of cavalry massed makes a fine target.

By dark that night the infantry objectives had not been gained, and at midnight we were withdrawn to Wailly, a village some four miles south of Arras. The whole division had to go back by the same track, for it was not possible to get along anywhere else, owing to the wire and trenches. I fell into a trench once, horse and all, and the packs were always in trouble.

My tool pack pony "Billy" fell into a shell-hole and never caught us up till next day. Twice I lost touch and did not know where we were, but somehow or other we kept on the right track. It was absolutely pitch dark and you couldn't see your hand in front of you. After about two hours we reached Wailly. where we were to bivouac. I was not sorry to finish that journey. It is no joke moving a large force of cavalry in the dark across broken country. The weather was terribly cold.

More snow had fallen and in addition there was a strong wind. I think that night was the most miserable I have ever spent. I slept behind my saddle, which gave a certain amount of shelter, but in the morning, I was covered with snow from head to foot. I had little sleep that night, and had to get up several times and walk about to keep warm. The horses had all been clipped out during the winter and had no rugs, so that they suffered terribly. Many died. The cheerfulness of the men under conditions like this is positively amazing: one never hears a murmur, except various uncomplimentary remarks about the weather. At dawn the next day I was woken up by two of them shouting some humorous remarks at each other at the top of their voices. A few fellows like that are absolutely invaluable.

At two o'clock next day we were brought up again and sent on to the jumping-off point which was between Neuville-Vitasse and Wancourt. This was an unpleasant journey. To reach the appointed spot we had to pass close to Wancourt village, which was still held by the Huns. The leading troops were met with heavy machine-gun fire from the village, which emptied some saddles and did considerable execution amongst the horses; but the chief danger was from the German gunners on the ridge behind, who had us in full view for several hundred yards before we reached the valley we were making for.

As it happened, a heavy blizzard came down just as the advance began, and this must have shielded the leading troops from view, but the rest of the brigade must have made a fine, if a fleeting, target seen against the snow. There was one cross-road which I shall not easily forget. A battery of field guns was beautifully ranged on to this, and this was one of the liveliest spots I remember. The brigade was scurrying down the hill at a fast pace with fifty yards' distance between troops. I saw one troop receive a shell right amongst them; and for a moment they were lost in smoke.

When the smoke cleared away, I saw a mass of mangled men and horses. I have grown accustomed to the sight of blood, and of men with limbs blown off, but a badly wounded horse is one of the most revolting sights I know. There was one horse lying right in the middle of the road with one foreleg blown right off and a huge gaping wound in its stomach from which its entrails were protruding.

Regimental headquarters got through with only two casualties, but most troops suffered considerably at that corner. My own mare "Kitty" was very excitable under fire and reared right up when some shells dropped near us, almost unseating me and

THIS WAS ONE OF THE LIVELIEST SPOTS I REMEMBER.

knocking off my steel helmet. If the Huns had fired more shrapnel, the casualties would have been very heavy: as it was they fired almost entirely H.E., a large proportion of which were "duds."

The point we had now reached was the infantry front line; and the Huns were just over a little rise. It is extraordinary how a small valley will hide a large force. Here was a brigade of cavalry with its R.H.A., etc., absolutely hidden in this small fold in the ground.

Then we had bad news: a reconnaissance to the front reported a broad trench, heavily wired, which was still held by the enemy. It was now dusk and useless to hope to do anything more that day, so we were withdrawn at dark to La Ronville, a suburb of Arras, where we drew much-needed rations and forage and got some sleep.

At 5 a.m. next day we returned to the valley whence we had just come, and here we waited for hours. Hopkins returned here and took over the adjutancy, and I returned to my squadron. During the morning I was sent with a patrol to reconnoitre Wancourt. This was an interesting job. I rode along up to the infantry outposts, who told me all they knew, and then worked round by the high ground to the south of the village. This high ground was still held by machine-guns, but from the point I had reached I could see a good many Huns moving about by a tall chimney behind the village.

There was also transport retiring eastwards. Corporal Goodheart, whose section I had taken with me for the reconnaissance, was tremendously excited. Some Huns kept passing between a house and the chimney, and we fired a few shots at them. I don't think we hit any, although Neame, my servant, swore he did; but at any rate we made one take to his heels and run. When he had gone about ten yards he fell, and we thought we had bagged him, but he got up again and disappeared behind the house. On the way back my mare fell into a trench and came over backwards with me. I was, however, none the worse, and brought back my report to the general.

I BROUGHT BACK MY REPORT

During the day, the 8th Cavalry Brigade on our left captured Monchy-le-Preux in cooperation with the infantry, but lost heavily in so doing, amongst the casualties being the brigadier.

After these two attempts to push us through we were not brought up again, but were withdrawn to Wailly, where we spent the night in the same field in the rain and snow. A lot more horses died from the cold, and hospital claimed a good many of the men.

I wonder how many people realise what it means to sleep out in the snow. Think of the saddlery, etc., lying in the slush. That night killed a lot more horses; the whole place was strewn with them in the morning. Neither I nor the men could sleep much, and most of us walked about half the night to keep warm. When dawn broke a queer sight met our eyes. Nearly every horse was covered with snow; many were lying down, unable to get up again.

Next day we were withdrawn to Gaudiempre, and later to billets along the Authuille River. So ended Arras for us. Many of our oldest soldiers said it was the greatest hardship they had undergone during the war.

Chapter 10

Billeting

One of the things which always caused more trouble, fuss and worry than anything else was billeting. Some people are experts at this game and never fail to get good billets. Others have the knack of never getting good ones. I think there is more "scrounging" and "pinching" in billeting than in anything else. It doesn't matter what your rank, or what your command: I have never met anyone who admitted that his billets were really good. There may not be much grousing in this line so high up as corps, since it is not often that a corps is out of the line all at the same time. I think the trouble begins at the division.

I know of many divisional commanders who were continually going to Corps H.Q. to make complaints about their billets: but I don't think that a division ever gets much "change" out of a corps. To start with, no high official likes to make too much of a fuss to his superiors. A divisional commander cannot say to a corps commander: "My billets are absolutely hopeless: for God's sake give me some others."

It is not until you come down as low as squadrons that you can really speak out.

The grousing begins with regiments. The surest way to upset a colonel is to put him in a rotten H.Q. The class of billet which he occupies can soon be guessed by his subordinates, according to what kind of temper he is in.

But the grousing after you are settled into billets is nothing like the fuss that people make about getting into them. It is the process of allotting the billets and putting the horses and men into them that is the real trouble.

We often read in books, "They went and billeted in such and such a village," but this cannot convey to the lay mind what really happens. I have explained that, when a regiment moves, a billeting party is always sent on ahead to arrange quarters in the new area. Whoever is in charge of the party—usually the second in command—allots an area to each squadron, and then the fun starts. Somehow or other there is always a house with a lot of accommodation on the edge of each area, and unless it has been specially laid down whose it is to be there is apt to be confusion. To be kept waiting in the daytime is never pleasant, but to stand about for an hour in the middle of the night, often in the rain, is apt to irritate people. I can remember more than one instance of this.

On one occasion my squadron and "B." Squadron had each thought that a certain house belonged to them. When the regiment arrived, I was told to take my troop in that farm. On reaching it I found that "B." Squadron were already in it, so I found the officer in charge and remonstrated with him.

"This is my billet," I said, feeling none too pleasantly disposed towards him.

"Rubbish, I was told distinctly to come here."

"So was I."

"But, my good fellow—"

"There is no 'but' about it. I mean—"

"Here, I'll go and see Hunt about it and ask him; he did the billeting and he must know."

Just then Rosy, who had done the billeting for us, arrived on the scene.

"All right?" he asked.

"All wrong," I replied coldly. "Nap here is in my billets."

"I tell you I am not in your billets," he said.

"I shall have to see Major Hunt," said Rosy, and off he went. While we were waiting Stephens arrived.

"What the blazes is all this muddle?" he growled. "Just like you, Delius, if anyone makes a 'box-up' it is sure to be you. You are not fit to lead a section, much less a troop; get your men in at once."

"But—" I protested.

"I want no 'buts,'" he roared, trembling with rage, "do what you are—"

Just then he spotted the "B." Squadron troop and realised that of course we could not help standing out in the road. However, I have learned not to mind being abused even when I am not to blame: two years in the army makes this kind of thing roll off you like water off a duck's back. In another minute Hunt and Thompson of "B." Squadron arrived, and there was a long discussion. Eventually it was decided that I was to have half the farm; other accommodation had been found for the rest of my troop and the other half of Nap's.

All this swearing and palavering took place before our men, but they get used to that. I have often been told that an officer should never be "told off" before his men, but as a matter of fact it does not matter a bit. If you have not sufficient personality to maintain your position just because you are called a d——d fool in front of your men, you must be ridiculously sensitive. Stephens has told me that he was once sent off parade by the colonel for having white girths on when he should have had blue ones. If you are cursed unjustly, as often happens, and your men think anything of you, you will have them on your side at once. Besides, it shows them that they are not the only people who come in for the damning and cursing. The officers are "for it" just the same, and probably more so.

Of course, it is very different with an N.C.O. It is absolutely criminal to tell off one of these in front of his men. You lower him at once. It is far harder for him to maintain his position than for you. Of course, at drill nothing matters; for this is simply one roar of abuse from start to finish, and it is all forgotten five minutes afterwards, when people become themselves again.

There is a class of person who cannot receive abuse without passing it on to those beneath him. He thinks it is the thing to do. But he is usually wrong. If you are cursed into heaps for something, it is generally your fault, and even if it is not it is far better to keep quiet. If one of your corporals has committed some atrocity, "bite" him afterwards when you have cooled down and are normal again. It is pitiable to see a man fly into a rage with his men just because he has been called an idiot— probably justly.

Of course, there are times when the men should be "bitten," but there is a right time and a wrong.

But I have wandered from my subject, which is billeting. On many occasions I did the billeting myself. It is really rather fun; there are certain things, however, to avoid. One of these is very important: *i.e.* when the squadron arrives, never tell the squadron leader that the accommodation is good; always say it is bad, and then he will expect nothing. Stephens was very fussy about billets, and Rosy, who usually did our billeting, was often abused quite unjustly.

An occasion I remember well was when coming back from Arras. Rosy was on leave so I had to do the job. At Barly the billets were good, but I knew better than to say so.

I met the squadron coming in and saluted the major.

"Well, what luck?" he asked.

"Not much," I replied. "About the worst place I have struck for ages."

"Why, what's the trouble?"

"Oh, hardly any horses under cover, and rotten sleeping accommodation both for officers and men."

"Oh, Lord! Well, never mind, I suppose we'll get in somehow."

"I'm afraid it will be pretty damnable," I said, hopelessly. "Still, we and the sergeants have a mess, and the men will at any rate be warm."

While the squadron was getting "fixed up" I took the major round to see the area.

"Oh, this isn't really so bad," he said looking into a fine barn for a dozen horses. "I thought you said that there were very few horses under cover."

"Well, as a matter of fact, each troop has a few under, and I dare say they have found some more places since I looked round myself."

"Where do the men of this troop sleep?"

"Each section has a room with a stove and some straw mattresses."

"Really, that sounds very nice."

"Yes, it is not as bad as I thought."

"Where is the mess?"

"Round here," I replied, leading the way into a large house standing back from the road.

"Ah, a *château*!"

"Well, not exactly, but it is a pretty decent looking place, and the *patron* is not a bad old stick."

We thereupon entered a nice room with a table, chairs, and a fire burning in the grate.

"Ah, this is first rate!" said the major. "You must be very particular if you call these bad billets."

"Well, perhaps I underrated them slightly, but I have seen better in my time. Of course, there are no sheets on your—"

"Sheets be damned!" he snapped. "Do you suppose I'm as particular as all that? You seem to think—"

I knew that I had now gone far enough; so, I went off to my troop and saw the horses groomed and fed. I should like to have said that it was because he was so *difficile* about billets that I always made a point of saying that they were hopelessly bad, but I think he understood all right.

The actual dealing with the inhabitants is rather fun. I acquired considerable skill in this line after a bit. It is wonderful what can be done by making yourself pleasant to old French men and women. Often you will come to a house where some sour-faced old woman will greet you.

"*Madame, avez vous place pour des chevaux?*"

"*Ah, non, il y a des vaches, et des cochons partout.*"

But surely *Madame* has room for two or three? Perhaps, at any rate, she could billet some men?

Ah, that is better, she will take three horses, and has a nice warm room for half a dozen men. That is splendid.

Farther on you see a house which might possibly have a mess, and a bedroom for *Monsieur le major*. *Monsieur* has his house full of *evacués*: sorry, *pas moyen*, but I ought to try the house opposite, where *Madame* has *beaucoup de place*. Eventually you find you have got room for everyone, and with any luck you will be able to wolf an omelette and a *tartine* before the regiment arrives.

If there is a town-major in the village everything is much easier, since he has a list of all houses where men and horses can be billeted. On the whole, however, this is a thankless job. No one appreciates the difficulties.

Sometimes you are not given your area until a few minutes before the arrival of the squadron. Then they have to wait, and that is the time when people call you all kinds of names.

When it is known that you are going to stay in an area for some time, H.Q. is usually bombarded with complaints about this, that and the other. One squadron thinks it has not enough room for its horses, another for its men, another cannot find a sergeants' mess, etc.

One usually finds H.Q. cold and unresponsive in these matters, especially when they are well off themselves: it is always easy to bear philosophically the troubles of other people.

One of the greatest nuisances a troop leader has to deal with is that of claims. An inhabitant may put in a claim for damages against the troops who have caused it. A great deal of *dégâts* are unavoidable; for instance, it is not your fault if your horses kick down part of a stable. For this kind of thing the government will pay, and each division has a claims officer whose sole job is to deal with such cases.

On the other hand, many cases of *dégâts* are not unavoidable. Naturally the government will not pay if you let your men help themselves to a farmer's hay or vegetables. This is the fault of the unit concerned, and they have to make the damage good.

There are, of course, inhabitants of various kinds. Some will put in a claim for the slightest thing, and even try to saddle you with the responsibility for things that you have never done. I have come across many like this. But happily, the majority are of the other kind and are only too ready to help you in every way. People are particularly civil in the districts which have been occupied by the Huns.

Chapter 11

Recuperating

The Arras show was terribly disappointing from our point of view, although broadly speaking it was a brilliant success. At a heavy price, especially in horses, we had achieved practically nothing. An infantry officer who was in the line near Wancourt when we swept down into the valley told me, however, that the moral effect of our presence was great. He had himself seen numbers of Boches pack up and run when we appeared. I have no doubt that we could have taken Wancourt, but I believe that this would have been the limit of our success, because the Hun had a prepared line the other side of the river.

If a wedge is to be driven into an enemy trench system, it must be done on a broad front; the deeper you drive the wedge the narrower it becomes because your flanks must be protected. The more men you use to protect your flanks, the narrower becomes your front, and you run the risk of creating a dangerous salient in your line if you do not bear this in mind.

The success achieved had certainly been greater than on the Somme in 1916, and we had to console ourselves with the thought that we were gradually coming nearer to gaining our ends.

In those days of heavy bombardments, it was practically impossible for horses to move across the shell-torn area except by a prepared track. I take off my hat to those who prepared the track at Arras, which necessitated the filling in or bridging of trenches, and the clearing of wire entanglements many yards in width.

The work on this occasion was done by some of our men who had been sent up dismounted beforehand; it had been done well and brought right up to the leading infantry under heavy fire.

Horses under fire are curious creatures: there are some which would not even wink an eye if a mine went up in front of them; there are others which go mad with fright at the crack of a bullet. In time most horses get used to it, but a steady horse is a great asset when you are trying to read a map, or giving or receiving orders during a show. "Kitty" was rather nervous under fire, and at times tried my temper sorely. She had a nasty habit of rearing absolutely straight up when thoroughly frightened.

Of course, the horses had fallen away terribly in condition during this operation, so that the natural sequel was a "horse-strafe." This was more pleasant than most, since the authorities sent us extra rations of hay and oats, and did everything possible to help us. In spite of the fine weather, however, which we enjoyed during May and the early part of June, the horses had not entirely recovered even by the autumn. A horse can lose condition in a few days, but it takes him months to put it on again.

We remained in billets until May 12th, when we moved off south to take over a sector of the line east of Péronne. The billets we were in on the Authuille were good and the country delightful; one village some miles off, Gueschart, was especially pretty, hidden away in a little wood now green with spring foliage. Our mess was close to the river, and we made a canoe in which we used to shoot the rapids under the bridge. On one occasion we capsised, an event which attracted a large crowd of civilians, and there was much applause when Stephens swarmed up one of the pillars of the bridge, soaked to the skin. Those were pleasant days.

Hunt took the junior officers out on some staff rides: the answer to most of his questions was "gallop." If you said this, you were usually more or less right.

He was a good instructor and had heaps of experience behind him.

The weather was so fine here that most of us slept outside.

My bivouac was raided on one occasion by some of the others, but I flatter myself that I repelled them with a sustained fire of stones and clods of earth. The poor man in whose garden I was sleeping did not appreciate the situation at all. He believed that some lawless set of bandits were raiding his potato patch and turned out, clad only in a shirt, to beat off the attackers. Encouraged by my abusive remarks about the assailants, he did excellent work with a broom, and the attack was repulsed. He was for going to the *mairie* and telling the local police, until I explained the situation, when he joined heartily in the joke.

I believe they thought us mad, these good French people.

CHAPTER 12

A Cricket Match

Our brigadier was a capital chap. Before the war he had commanded a regiment in India, and had been appointed to our brigade in 1915.

I shall not easily forget a concert which we gave in his honour. He was rather bald, and of this our colonel was not slow to take advantage in his opening speech, which was as follows:

> Gentlemen, we are giving a concert tonight in honour of our new brigadier. Now there is no need to be frightened of a general: the only people who are so, are very old colonels and very young subaltern officers. Amongst other points I must ask you to note that the barrenness of the outside of his head is no indication of what is inside.

Colonel Hewitt and the general had known each other long before the war, and were, I believe, great friends. I do not remember the rest of the speech, but this much has always stuck in my mind.

The brigade major too was a great sportsman, and a thoroughly efficient staff officer: he was much liked by everyone except adjutants who could not get their returns in at the proper time. He was no friend to these.

I have heard a lot about the relations between regimental and staff officers. I know heaps of people who abuse the latter and say that they do nothing to help the regiments. But this point of view is largely due to ignorance. You often hear people say:

"Why don't the staff do this, or that," or "You never see our staff up in the line." If the cause of these complaints were inquired into, you would usually find that there is an excellent reason for everything. After all, the place of the staff is not in the front line. Their business is to run the show from the rear. No man can be in two places at once, and if they spent their time in the firing line there would soon be plenty of grousing about things that were not going right. Our staff, at any rate, was in the front line as much as, if not more than, necessary, and no one could have looked after us better. Of course, there are occasions when things go wrong, but the fault often lies with someone far remote in the chain of responsibility.

The person who comes in for most abuse is the staff captain. He is the man responsible for billets and supplies, two very important things. Nothing makes people grumble more than bad billets and poor rations. The first things that people say when they find themselves in rotten billets is: "What a hopeless staff captain we have got." Poor unfortunate fellow! It is not usually his fault. He is given an area by the division and cannot make it bigger than it is.

But the real cause of any grousing against the staff is the thought that they are comfortably installed in some *château* while the regiments are marching in bad weather or sitting in water-logged trenches. The "*château*" grouse is usually based on a fallacy. If there happens to be a *château* handy it would be foolish not to go into it. Anyone will admit that. Besides many regimental officers think that a staff job necessarily involves a "cushy" time. It is not so at all. Anyone who has seen an H.Q. at work during an advance or a retreat will tell you that, even if it is in a *château*, many of the staff officers do not get a wink of sleep. I have had a taste of this kind of thing, both as adjutant and for a short time as staff captain.

It depends entirely on a man's character whether he is fitted for regimental or staff work. There are some men who make first-rate leaders of men, but who would make hopeless staff officers. The reverse is also true. I believe that a staff officer is all the better if he has been a good regimental officer. The greater part of our staff have been regimental officers, and most of them have done their bit in the line. I know that there are many people who have sat in "cushy" jobs in England the whole war; but there are many regimental officers in this flock as well as staff.

Our brigadier encouraged all games and sports very strongly. He used to play cricket himself and was a googly bowler of no mean talent. In one match I saw him take no less than six wickets. He would have taken seven had I not missed a sitting catch at mid-off.

Cricket in France is distinctly amusing. We had divisional, brigade, regimental, squadron, and even troop matches. The two former revealed some players of considerable ability. We mustered several old blues and county players, and I believe the Divisional XI. would have taken on a good Free Forester side. But the most entertaining games were the inter-squadron and troop matches. The British cavalryman is not as a rule a brilliant cricketer; he has, on the other hand, a good eye, and is capable of remarkably fast bowling and colossal hitting. The roughness of the grounds contributed largely to the uncertainty of these games.

My troop shoeing-smith was one of the fastest bowlers I have ever seen. He stood about six feet three in his socks, and had arms like a Hercules. His bowling was decidedly Prussian in its frightfulness, for he took a run of about thirty yards and delivered the ball while running at top speed. Most fast bowlers are tired after a few overs, but he liked to go on bowling throughout an innings and was, in fact, quite hurt if he was taken off.

Corporal Palmer was a bowler of a very different kind. He bowled "googlies" of the most cunning type. The amount of work that he got on to the ball was astonishing. He had, however, one great fault: he became seized by an ungovernable rage if he was hit about. His bad temper when playing cricket was well known to the rest of the team, who used to badger him when he lost his "hair." Had he had more self-control, he would have made a fine cricketer.

One match we had against another troop was especially

amusing. The other side went in first, and were actually out for 17 runs. Johnson, my shoeing-smith, and Corporal Palmer were too much for our opponents. Our innings was more successful. Two of my stonewallers who went in first put up 15 before they were separated, although this took 45 minutes. Then followed a collapse. This was started by a man being run out. It happened as follows: Wilson, a slogger, hit a ball hard to cover-point—an unusual direction since most hits were towards square leg—his partner thinking the ball was past, began to run and had just reached the other end when cover-point picked up the ball. Then a tragedy occurred: both the batsmen, who were now at Wilson's end, for some inexplicable reason dashed for the other end. This led to wild shouting by the supporters of both sides.

Cover-point was so bewildered that he did not know which end to throw. Eventually he threw straight and hard, and the ball struck Wilson's partner on the back of the neck just as he gained the crease. This probably saved his wicket, although he had to go to hospital next day, but the wicket-keeper threw the ball up to the other end and Wilson was run out. There was much arguing about this, since each said it was the other's fault, and the whole game was stopped for several minutes. After this, wickets fell rapidly until Sergeant Coates went in. He always went in last, as he said he was a stonewaller. He certainly was, for it took twenty minutes to shift him, although he only made one run. Our score was only 21 altogether. The scoring never was high.

Although we had pads and gloves, the men showed a great reluctance to put these on. When asked why, their usual answer was that they "wouldn't be out there long." They would rather get their shins banged and bruised than put on a pad. Another curious thing about soldier cricketers is their dread of left-hand bowling. I have never been able to understand this. They believe that there is something uncanny about it, and the moral effect of a left-hander is terrific.

They were great fun those cricket matches. We used to buy lettuces, buns, salmon, fruit, etc., and take tea out for both elevens. The ground was about two miles from our billets. We used to ride out there, bring the tea on a pack-pony, and lay the table in the garden of a farmhouse close by, the owner of which lent us plates, cups, knives, and all the crockery we wanted. These were enjoyable days.

Occasionally some dramatic events took place: on one occasion one of our officers bowled General Greenly out for "specs." I think this must have been the explanation of his uncertain temper just afterwards, for the next day some unit of the division got a fearful "raspberry" at an inspection.

Games have a tremendous effect upon the men's spirits, especially if the officers take part. In this way their minds are taken away from horses and soldiering for a short time. After all, the men have few amusements, and it is the duty of officers to provide them with recreation of all sorts when life is dull.

Nothing is worse than to let men become stale. This state of affairs can easily be avoided: there are dozens of ways of arousing their interest. If nothing is done to counteract boredom, they gradually lose interest in their work, in their horses, and themselves; their moral deteriorates, and this in time leads to loss of self-respect and finally crime. This state of affairs is easily avoided by games; it is especially true in the cavalry, which in this war has often been out of the line for several months on end.

CHAPTER 13

In the Line East of Péronne

On May 12th we left billets and marched south. Our route was practically the same as that which we had followed when we went down to the offensive on the Somme in 1916. After leaving Corbie we went on through Bray to Suzanne, where we stopped one night. The next day we marched across the old battlefield to Péronne and on to Tincourt, where we bivouacked.

To me there is something peculiarly fascinating about the desolation of the old Somme battlefields. You can stand on the top of a ridge anywhere and see on all sides of you the vast, gently rolling, lonely country. Every yard there is a shell-hole or a bit of old trench. As far as the eye can reach there is not a village standing: Combles, Suzanne, Sailly-Saillisel, Le Transloy, Rancourt, and many others lie before you in absolute and complete ruin. In some it is true to say that not one stone is left standing on another.

Perhaps at your feet, as you stand, there is an old trench with the remains of a bomb store or some tattered bits of uniform.

You cannot help thinking what that trench represents. To me it recalls the hundreds of days that men sat there when it was the front line; the agony of two years of trench warfare. You think of the dark, rainy nights when men lay there on fire-step huddled up in a cloak and a waterproof sheet, the wiring party which planted the pickets and ran out the wire between them. You think of the thousands of star-shells which have been fired from it, and of the sentry peering out into the darkness. How much human suffering it has seen!

Possibly it is an old communication trench. How many men have passed up and down it, you wonder, since it came into being. You think of the long chain of men coming up to relieve those in the line, and of the hundreds of ration-parties, etc., which have struggled along it in the mud. There, perhaps, are the remains of the dug-out where Company Headquarters was, with its ramshackle old table. There is the corner where the telephone used to stand. It was several months since the tide of battle had passed away from here; since then not a living being had been here. The sides of the trench are probably already crumbling and grass is beginning to grow all over it. Few of us guessed then that this hard-won country would again hear the roar of guns, and again see the German hordes come sweeping over it before a year had passed.

Péronne before the war must have been a beautiful place. It lies right on the banks of the Somme. The river is very wide here and broadens out into a kind of lake. Now the place lies practically in ruins: it had been largely burned by the Germans in their retirement, and scores of houses are just a heap of rubble and black beams.

On the left, as you come into the square going eastwards, is a shop with Félix Potin's sign-board still up. It was already well stocked with bread, vegetables, eggs, butter, etc., and was later on a godsend to our men. You could even get the *Daily Mail* there.

Tincourt, where our camp was to be, lies about five miles east of Péronne and about the same distance from the line. The country round is slightly more hilly than farther west, and less monotonous. Just beyond Tincourt lies the little hamlet of Boucly. There had been a magnificent *château* here, but this had shared the fate of all buildings in the district and now lay a heap of ruins.

The havoc wrought by the Huns in their retreat was appalling. Naturally the destruction of anything and everything which could possibly be of value to an enemy was to be expected, but much of no military significance had been destroyed as well.

Every village had been razed to the ground; every house had been blown up by a mine and left a heap of ruins. No one returning could find their old home with any certainty. Fruit trees had been felled, or ringed just sufficiently to ensure their dying; wells had been fouled; mines and factories laid flat and their machinery either sent away to Germany or else left in a tangled inextricable heap.

It is a fearful thought—the hundreds of villages ruined in this way, especially when one thinks of the thousands of families who are now homeless. I once saw an old woman returning to the home from which she had been driven in 1914. But what a sight met her eyes! All she found was a heap of bricks and broken beams. She burst into tears, just as many of these gallant French-women have when they saw the work of the Huns. Almost all these people have lost husbands or sons in the war, and many have lost their homes as well.

I have often thought of the horror of a war in England. Suppose one of our counties laid waste in this way: every town robbed of anything of value and then burned to the ground; all our cosy country villages left in ruins without a sign of life remaining; the smiling country-side left without a tree; and the forests all cut down for timber and sent off to a foreign country. God forbid that such a fate should ever overtake us.

On May 18th we formed a dismounted party and marched up through Roisel and St. Émilie to Epehy, where guides from the troops in the line met us. The warfare here was of a very different kind from that which obtained at Vermelles and Ypres. Along the ridge in front of us ran the great Hindenburg line, which was the enemy's main position; it had an incredible quantity of barbed wire in front of it and was a formidable obstacle. Along the valley between this line and the British trenches ran the St. Quentin Canal, and west of this the Germans had a line of outposts. Our position was a similar one; our main line was about a mile east of Epehy, and in front of this a number of small posts had been established. The two outpost lines were anything from 300 yards to a mile apart.

The comparatively great distance between the lines necessitated a lot of patrolling at night, and every evening at dusk a number of officers' and N.C.Os' patrols went out towards the German lines to listen for any sign of a raid or attack, and to report on anything of interest that the Huns might be doing.

It is a curious feeling being out half a mile or more in front of one's own trench where you can hear, and on clear nights even see, the Boches working. On such occasions you have to keep your eyes and ears open, for the Hun also has patrols out. The Boche patrols were usually fifteen or twenty strong. We began by sending out parties of six and seven men, but later our patrols were always stronger than this. Sometimes we used to meet the Huns out there in the dark, when short, sharp conflicts would take place.

On one occasion Corporal Moore came across a patrol of the enemy approaching our wire. He immediately rushed them, killing the officer and two Huns and capturing another. This little affair caused a tremendous noise. The German officer saw our party first and shouted "Hands up" in very good English. Corporal Moore's reply was to empty his revolver into him and charge the rest of the party; some of whom scattered. Then followed a lot of firing and bomb throwing, and the sound of this mingled with the shouts of both sides brought others of our patrols to the spot, besides reinforcements from the trenches behind. Sergeant Hogg slew a couple of Boches with his bayonet as they were trying to escape. Our casualties were only two wounded. The affair was a pretty lively one while it lasted.

I have never seen two such extraordinary looking people as our two prisoners. One was well over six feet in height, wore spectacles, and was as thin as a rake. His neck resembled closely that of a giraffe. Another peculiar thing about him was the size of his feet, which were some of the largest I had ever seen. He had lost his cap in the struggle, and a large piece of cloth had been torn out of the seat of his breeches. His face was all plastered with mud, and altogether he made a pretty picture.

He explained that he tried to resist, but was unable to do

so, since one of our men had jumped on to him while he was crawling in the long grass and had crushed the wind out of him. The other was a little round fellow and as smart as could be. He was very annoyed at being captured, and was loud in his abuse of Corporal Moore who had collared him by the neck from behind. He said their patrol had been twelve strong. Ours was only seven, so that the affair reflected great credit on Corporal Moore. He was awarded the Military Medal for his work.

After some days in this sector we came out of the line into reserve, and later took over another part of the line near Ronssoy. The conditions were much the same here as where we had come from. Just on the left of the sector held by us was the house known as Gillemont Farm. Here a German post was only some hundred yards from one of ours. One night the squadron there decided to raid the enemy trench.

Elaborate preparations were made and "zero" fixed for 2 a.m. on a certain day. The troops on either side were informed of the raid, and every one eagerly awaited zero hour. The attack was preceded by a violent bombardment of four minutes by Heavy Artillery, Field Artillery, R.H.A., trench mortars, etc., after which the attackers rushed across into the enemy's post. The wire had been well cut by the bombardment so that there was little difficulty in reaching it. Then followed a few minutes of killing. Forty Huns were killed and twelve captured, and brought back in triumph.

It is always amusing to see the coloured rockets which the Boches send up as signals to their artillery or headquarters. These can be red, green, golden rain, or almost any colour, and are changed from time to time so that we do not know with any certainty what each signal means. On this occasion a rocket bursting into two red balls was fired almost as soon as our bombardment started; this was answered by another further back in the German lines.

Then other German units apparently getting jumpy took it up. But the artillery response was very feeble and did not come for some time. When it did come the raid was over. The Boches put over a few "whizzbangs" on to our trenches, and some how-itzers a long way back coughed up a few 5.9s, which dropped into Ronssoy behind us, and then all was quiet again, and no sound could be heard except the distant rumble of limbers and the occasional plop of the Very Lights.

When we were in reserve, I used to wander about the gardens of the villages round. In some I found asparagus beds, strawber-ries, lettuces, peas, beans, and all kinds of fruits and vegetables. There were some lovely rose gardens too which were still flour-ishing, although neglected and overgrown with weeds and grass.

So, we spent the summer. The same kind of warfare went on day after day; but it is less monotonous to occupy detached posts than to sit in the same trench for weeks without being able to move. Here one could move about almost anywhere without being seen. Besides, it was fine summer weather, and the coun-try, although devastated, preserved still a lot of its beauty. The fields in which were our trenches were covered with long luxu-riant grass waiting to be made into hay.

All the sights and sounds of summer in the country were there: dozens of swallows flitted about, and the air was alive with the humming of insects and the murmur of innumerable bees. There were quantities of butterflies, including peacocks, swal-low-tails, red-admirals, and hundreds of common whites and browns. One missed, however, the farms and the lowing herds which had dotted the countryside three years ago.

During the latter part of this time in the line I was again employed as adjutant. The adjutant in trench warfare is a busy man. His chief duty is to deal with all the correspondence and orders which come in; he must prepare the necessary returns for the commanding officer to sign, and despatch these to the bri-gade. The brigade requires simply dozens of these: for instance, you have to send a situation report twice daily, also a wind re-port every few hours, a work return showing improvements to trenches, new trenches dug, wire put up, etc. They also want to know what patrols were out the night before, what they saw or heard, and what patrols are going out next night.

Besides this, you have to send them your daily strength, and your casualty report; all these returns have to be in at fixed hours. It is not easy to collect them. All this necessitates a lot of writing for the squadron leaders in the front line, and writing in the front line is done under difficulties. Another point of importance is that all this writing robs people of a lot of sleep, and sleep is a thing of which everyone in the line must have as much as possible.

But the bane of the adjutant's life is the telephone. Telephones are installed in all our trench systems: headquarters is usually connected to all the squadrons and to the brigade. It is the brigade which is such a bore: every minute they want something. But it is not their fault for they have to supply the information required by the division. There is something diabolical about military telephones or about soldiers who use telephones. The instrument usually ceases to function just when you are getting on. This causes you to wait often for ages. When you are connected again both parties are somewhat irritated.

The brigade major or staff-captain—for it is usually he—is vexed because possibly you have sent in a return half an hour late; the uncertainty of the telephone has vexed him more, and you are yourself probably somewhat annoyed at being woken up. Military telephone conversations are usually short, sharp and abusive. Sometimes you want to get something out of the brigade. Then you must coax and flatter them; but the other kind of conversation is the more common.

I believe the adjutant gets less sleep than anyone; besides his other duties he must go round and see the squadrons and find out what they require; he must go and worry the brigade to get these requirements. He must also accompany the C.O. when he walks round; in fact, he has a pretty busy time.

Our H.Q. was in a quarry some two hundred yards behind the line. Part of the bank had been cut away and shelters made with timber and corrugated iron. We had a nice little mess, with a table and benches. There was also an orderly room; this was most necessary as documents and papers accumulate at an almost incredible rate.

From our lines one could often see the Boches walking about in the distance. There was a village in front called La Terrière, which was just behind the Hindenburg line. Here I often saw the Huns working, carrying planks, and material for building purposes. The range was too great for sniping with rifles, but occasionally we used to get the gunners on to them. Then the Boches used to take cover, and come out again perhaps in half an hour. One day we sniped them with a sixty-pounder. A great shell landed right amongst their working party. I never saw the result on account of the smoke and dust, but they did not come out again that day.

Dawn was usually the best time to see them in most places: at this hour one could sometimes do some good sniping with rifles. We used to see the last of the working parties returning to their trenches after the night's work. Sometimes I saw fat, round Huns wheeling barrows or hand-carts full of tools, rations, etc. Dawn was the signal for cease work. It was not a case of man going forth to his labour until the evening, but exactly the reverse.

One of the chief amusements was the passing of a train, the smoke of which was often visible behind the German lines. This passed every morning about dawn and appeared amongst the woods behind Bony, a village in front of us. Someone christened it the Bony Express. We, of course, told our gunners about it, and one or more batteries used to lay wait for it. When it appeared, they used to fire for all they were worth. Every day some gunner said that his battery bagged it, but nevertheless it always appeared the next day at the same time and place. Sometimes it used to whistle as though in defiance.

One night the Boches attempted a raid on one of our posts. At about 1 a.m. they fired a coloured rocket and immediately afterwards the Boche guns opened. Our machine-guns opened a vigorous fire into the darkness, and this, coupled with our rifle fire, must have stopped them from coming on with any determination, for only about a dozen came up to our wire; none got through it, and most of them were driven off, leaving two prisoners in our hands.

When the "shoot" opened the C.O. and I were just returning from visiting the posts. We had a lively journey back to H.Q., for the 200 yards of road which separated the trenches from headquarters just came in nicely for the Hun barrage.

The telephone office was a fine sight when I arrived. The brigade hearing the noise were asking what it was all about; I was just telling them when the wire was cut by a shell; we could not get on to the squadrons, as all these lines were cut also. It was really quite amusing. Our signallers were splendid on that occasion; they went out and got visual communication with lamps, and several messages came through. It is not an easy thing to send, receive, and write down messages in the dark in the middle of a barrage.

The shell fire caused some fifteen casualties; it was pretty lively while it lasted, but it was all over in ten minutes.

Sentries sometimes say and do humorous things, consciously and unconsciously. I once heard the following conversation:

"'Alt, who goes there!"

"12th blinkin' Lancers."

"Pass, 12th blinkin' Lancers."

On another occasion I saw a sentry fire off a Very Light into the parapet of his trench by mistake; the flare burst there and gave a very bright light just as if it had been in the air. Three men were sleeping close to the place when this happened. I suppose that they thought that it was some new form of frightfulness, for the unfortunate fellows suddenly woke up, leapt out of their shelter and tripped over a brazier which was standing in the trench; the brazier was upset, and the unfortunate three fell flat into the mud. They had something to say to that sentry; in fact, they gave him some information about himself which he cannot have possessed before.

Life back with the horses was no sinecure: when you have only five or six men left to look after thirty horses, it is no joke. Back there every one was in tents or home-made bivouacs of felt or corrugated iron. One can make oneself extraordinarily comfortable with a little trouble.

Towards the end of July, the division left for the Frévent-St.-Pol area. It was a pleasant change to get back to civilization again. We had not seen a civilian for over two months.

CHAPTER 14

Life in Billets

The conditions in which we lived in France tended to make *esprit de squadron* very strong. *Esprit de regiment* was of course great as well; but I believe that the former was far the stronger.

This is really natural, because with squadrons each in separate villages, often two or three miles away from each other, one often saw very little of them. Even troops were sometimes a long way apart. The result was a tremendously strong *esprit de troop*, stronger than it ever could be in peace-time. The men of a troop keep much to themselves—just like boys of the same house at a public school. It is not often that one sees three or four men of different troops walking together; not that they are unsociable, but that the conditions and situation of their billets make each unit keep much to itself.

This feeling is, to a slight extent, prevalent amongst the officers. When I first came out, we were three miles from the other squadrons, and it was a long time before I got to know the other officers. In winter especially, when the weather and the roads are bad, one hardly ever saw the other squadrons.

I do not think this is good for anyone. One tends, if one is not careful, to get into a groove, from which it is not easy to get out. No one is the worse for seeing other people and hearing their ideas and what they have got to say. One must be very careful not to become narrow-minded, and to think that no one can be right except oneself.

In billets no one likes to be near headquarters. In a way it is a natural feeling: the idea underlying most people's minds is that the colonel might be continually prying round and saying that this or that is wrong, or that a certain thing must be done at once. This feeling applies to all headquarters up to a certain height. I should not like to have my troop billeted in front of the officer's mess, nor would a section leader like to have his stable straight opposite his troop leader's window. I have heard officers of higher rank than most people would believe express these very sentiments. Everybody, no matter of what rank, has a certain amount of natural and reasonable dread of the person above him.

But although headquarters *chastise the wicked*, they must also be looked on as the place where good and necessary things are to be got. Theoretically, I know, every part of a unit should be treated alike, and that everything that is got is divided equally. But I don't believe that anyone will deny that the people who are on the best terms with their superiors are usually better looked after than the others. I know perfectly well that if a squadron leader goes and dines with the colonel occasionally, or goes out shooting with him, etc., somehow or other he will get what he wants more easily' than another who keeps aloof and thinks that Headquarters do nothing to help him.

It is human nature again: I know of colonels who were always visiting Brigade H.Q., dining with the general or going pig-sticking with him, and of adjutants who were continually cultivating the acquaintance of the brigade major and the staff captain. I am absolutely convinced that it makes all the difference in the world.

Look at it from the superiors' point of view, beginning low down on the ladder. If a section leader of mine kept absolutely aloof, and regarded the troop sergeant or myself as beings who were there not to help, but to say that everything was wrong, rather than as a person from whom to ask advice and help, I could not have taken the same interest in him and his affairs as in one whose outlook was of the other kind. This is only a human feeling after all. It is just the same higher up the scale.

Of course, a great deal depends on the nature of your superior. There are some who are out to help you in every way they can; there are, unfortunately, others who do not care a fig about the welfare of those below them.

The billets near Frévent were not at all bad. The weather was sunny and warm and the horses thrived: the inhabitants were really friendly, with one or two exceptions. I spoke a certain amount of French, and had learnt a good deal during the time I had been in France, so that I never had much difficulty in getting what I wanted.

My French was of enormous value to me; my troop also benefited by it, since I was able to get things out of the inhabitants which I could not have got had I only known a few words. If you can speak fairly well and coax and humour the people you can get heaps of things. I have met crusty old men and sour old women who were as stingy as could be, but by a little coaxing and flattering I have usually managed to get what I wanted. Being on good terms with these people is very important; some things of course can be requisitioned, but I seldom had to have recourse to this method. It was always advisable to avoid it if you could.

During our stay in this district we had quite a lot of amusement. The hospital at Frévent had a fine cricket-ground, and we played several matches on this. Our brigadier played as usual. He seemed to be somewhat displeased with the fielding of the Brigade XI., and threatened to have us out for fielding practice. He did once or twice: he used to hit "skiers" for us to catch. Most of these were caught during the practices, but the ones I saw hit during a match were put on to the floor.

During August I had leave, and had a capital time. Leave had been increased to ten days; the extra three days made a huge difference. You just have time to make arrangements. Later it was increased to a fortnight and this was bliss.

A lot of regiments held sports and races during the summer; these were capital fun. There were mounted hurdle-races for all ranks, as well as tent-pegging, jumping, and many dismounted events. Jumping in a competition is a good experience for anybody. If you feel at all nervous, it is just like going in to bat before a large crowd. Besides, you are performing before a professional audience. No one is more critical than soldiers. At these sports there was usually a clown who performed all kinds of tricks, and used to make a fool of anyone who fell off or committed any atrocities.

But the races were the best fun. In these generals, colonels, captains, subalterns participated alike. Amongst the competitors were some who had ridden many races before the war, and some who had never ridden one before. Our colonel was very keen on this sort of thing and rode in all the races himself. The most comical part was the start. We were formed up in line just like a troop, only with a front of thirty-five instead of seventeen. We drew for places and our brigadier let the flag drop. Once, I believe, our colonel jockeyed me out of my rightful place; but as I finished before him, I did not mind much. These races were watched by almost all the men of the brigade and much enthusiasm was shown.

There were also all kinds of mounted races for the men, and in these my servant used to perform with some success. He was especially good in such things as the V.C. race. The competitors gallop half a mile over various obstacles, dismount, pick up a dummy representing a wounded man, and ride back with it across the front of the saddle. Someone usually falls off during this performance. That is what the men like more than anything.

Amongst the dismounted events, one of the favourites is the "greasy pole." In this, two men sit opposite each other on a pole smeared with grease, or some slippery substance, suspended across a ditch full of water. Both are armed with sandbags, and at a given signal try to knock each other off the pole into the water. Sometimes one or the other loses his balance, and you would expect him to fall into the ditch any moment. But the tenacity of the British soldier is proverbial; it even extends to this pastime. I once saw a man hanging on by his toes with his head dangling in the water. With his hands he reached the legs of his opponent and by a sudden twist actually pitched him into the ditch, when the latter thought that victory lay in his grasp.

Another popular sport was wrestling on horseback: teams of four men stripped to the waist and riding bareback were set against each other. Of course, the secret of success is having a quiet horse. I have seen some fine acrobatic feats performed in this event, men creeping along the horse's belly, etc. Anyone who touched the ground was "out." Anything was allowed except catching hold of an opponent by the hair, which was barred. On one occasion several of the horses, terrified by this unusual form of equitation, bolted and carried their riders off, sitting in every conceivable position. Some were sitting on back to front, others hanging underneath, etc.

The remainder of the summer passed pleasantly by. In October we marched up to St. Pol; we were told we were *en route* for Paschendaele, where the ridge had been all but gained. I suppose the idea was a cavalry sweep along the Belgian plains to Zeebrugge, Ostend, Bruges, etc. Unfortunately, it never came off.

1917 had been a disappointing year for us. After all, what had we done? We had attempted a break through at Arras, but from the cavalry point of view nothing valuable had been achieved. We had held a part of the line for two months in the summer, but so far that was all. I think this thought depressed a good many people: one began to feel that here were five divisions of the finest troops in the world unable to justify their existence. Trained up to the pitch and straining at the leash to be "loosed," we had not had a real opportunity. Instead of that, many of our best men had been killed or wounded in the various sectors of the line which we had held.

A cavalryman to me is the most gallant thing in the world when he has his saddle between his knees, but the sight of him on foot, ploughing through a foot of mud, with waders on instead of *puttees* and spurs, was enough to depress anyone. Besides, constant fatigues behind the line did a lot to crush the cavalry spirit. I knew that it was necessary that we should have to do the work, since, if we did not, it would mean that someone else would have to. Still the outlook was not a pleasant one.

A great many officers now wished to transfer to infantry, tanks, R.A.F., etc., since the prolonged inactivity was extremely irksome. Besides, no one likes to see and hear of the death of many of one's best pals, while one is sitting doing nothing, except looking after horses.

But the powers that be did not approve of these applications for transfer to other arms. A few officers and N.C.Os. were allowed to go, but very few. There was much grousing about this, but a memo, was sent round explaining that the cavalry must be maintained and that the C.-in-C. would not sanction the transfer of any more cavalry officers and men to other arms of the service. That put the lid on it: everyone had to stay where he was whether he liked it or not.

Looking after horses, week after week, is apt to become boring. No one likes these animals more than I, but with the continued "strafes" and "wheezes," etc., one gets desperately sick of them. Packs, too, take a lot of looking after. However, I have already expressed my views on this matter, so I will not say any more.

But no one need waste their time in billets, even if there is nothing doing. No one is any the worse for reading. There is heaps to be learned about soldiers and soldiering from books. The knowledge thus gained only becomes of real value when combined with practical experience, but reading is a great help.

CHAPTER 15

Cambrai—Bourlon Wood

At the end of October, the regiment had settled down into billets just outside Amiens. Here we fully expected to remain, with dismounted parties in the line. But rumours soon began to circulate that something was coming off. It soon became obvious that some "stunt" was in the air. Everything was kept secret. Guessing, however, that we should probably move at very short notice, I took the precaution to get my troop fitted out as far as possible, and have everything ready. On November 16th we received orders that the regiment was to move on the 17th. That night we marched to Bray-sur-Somme, where we remained until 4 p.m. the next day, when we moved on to Trefcon.

A night march is not a pleasant thing, especially when the column is a long one. However good the march discipline, you cannot avoid trotting "all out" one minute and the next running into the tail of the people in front of you, and stopping dead. On this march my tool-pack got into a ditch and never caught up until the next day. How I cussed those infernal packs. I expect the pack leader cursed it even more.

Here we learned what the "stunt" was. A surprise attack was coming off near Cambrai on the 21st, in which we were to be employed. We moved from Trefcon at 2 a.m. on the 21st. It was absolutely pitch dark and it took a great deal of time and trouble to get the squadron saddled up and on parade. Some even had gone so far as to say that the movement of a force of cavalry in the pitch dark was impossible. Experience, however, has shown that the British soldier can go anywhere and do anything, when he really sets out with the intention of doing it.

About 6 a.m. the brigade reached St. Emilie, where the horses were watered and fed. The bombardment was due to start at 6.20 and the attack at 6.30. Everyone waited the opening of the show with intense excitement. It opened with a crash and a roar which could be heard for miles. A few seconds afterwards the whole horizon was illuminated by scores of red rockets, the German S.O.S. signal. These flares, coupled with the myriads of gun flashes, the whole against a background of pink and grey sky, formed a most fascinating picture.

The 1st Cavalry Division was in front of us, and was to pass through as soon as the infantry had gained certain objectives. If the attack was a real success, more cavalry was to be passed through.

About 7 o'clock we moved on to Villers Faucon, where we stayed until midday. At that hour we moved off at a fast trot to a spot about half-way down the valley which runs from La Vacquerie to Masnières. The infantry and tanks had reached their objectives and some cavalry had gone through. Several villages had been captured and also guns and prisoners; some of the gunners had actually been charged and killed with the sword. But our division was not to support the leading division: the authorities had decided otherwise, and we were kept in that valley all night. It was a vile place; the weather also was atrocious. It blew and rained and snowed, and I am sure that it was one of the most unpleasant nights I have spent out here. At 2 a.m. we were ordered to saddle up and were told that we were moving back; when we were nearly ready the order was cancelled. This on the top of the shortage of rations, and the depth of the snow and mud, made us feel fairly miserable.

On the 22nd we went back to Villers Faucon. Here our lives were saved by the 55th Infantry Division, who gave us all manner of good things—officers, men and all. They gave a concert next day, but in the middle of this an officer got on to the platform and announced:

"All officers and men of the 2nd Cavalry Division are to return to their units at once, saddle up and prepare to move."

That night we marched to Fins, where we got a few hours' sleep before daylight.

It was still bitterly cold and cover was scanty; our bivouac was inches deep in mud, so that no one felt particularly cheerful.

Here we remained until the 28th, when we marched up to Ribecourt, and received orders to tell off a dismounted party to go into the line.

So, this was the finish of our expectations: we had expected a fine mounted show, and here we were forming a trench party for the *n*th time.

About 3 p.m. we moved off on foot some 200 strong, and spent the night in some dugouts by the side of the road, about half-way between Ribecourt and Bourlon Wood. It snowed heavily during the night. Here we remained the whole of the next day and left for Bourlon Wood at 9 p.m. The wood lay on the ridge about 2½ miles in front of us. We lost the way three times in the dark, and eventually reached the wood after a march of almost three hours. It was a fearful journey. When we got fairly close up to the wood we came in for some shelling.

The casualties were not many, as most of the shells landed amongst our Hotchkiss and tool packs behind. Some of these unfortunate ponies were killed, and others broke loose and galloped over the country. You can imagine how nice it is to chase loose horses about in the dark. Many of them were never seen again. We took up a position in the eastern outskirts of the wood; there was no trench, and the Germans were lining the road just at the top of Bourlon village. For the moment everything was quiet.

The first thing to do was to dig a trench; this was not easy as all our tools had gone west. We, however, made some scratches with bayonets. My servant was simply splendid on this occasion: he found an old broken German shovel, and went about digging a hole for most of the troop, asserting loudly that it would need a clever Hun to spot us in the morning. He was a great character in the troop and was much liked by the men; he was also a humourist and used to shout and sing at the top of his voice when things were at their worst. I had to tell him to moderate his voice here, as I felt sure that every Hun for miles would hear him.

Stephens was very keen on our digging in. He was right too, for when it got light, I saw that the people on our right were still in the open and were getting shot one by one. A sniper can make excellent practice at 200 yards even at a man lying down. The Huns opposite appeared to have no proper trench either, and moved about pretty freely until we began to let drive at them. Cole, one of my men, "picked off" their officer beautifully. A year afterwards I saw the place where he had fallen and his grave just beside it.

That day and the next the Huns let drive shells of all calibres on to our position. Lots of them seemed to strike tree trunks direct, and great trees used to come crashing down all over the wood. One of our men was crushed to death in this way. During the evening of the 29th the shelling was very heavy, and included a lot of gas. We had to stay with our gas masks on for hours. There was also a very heavy barrage on the ground behind the wood. We were relieved that night by a battalion of Londons, who told us that they had had 108 casualties coming in. But we were not to get away very lightly either. Saunders, one of our officers was killed, and poor Stephens badly wounded in the head and blinded in one eye. A lot of N.C.Os. and men were also hit.

That day was a bad one for "C" Squadron, for the loss of Stephens meant a lot to us. True, he rejoined in the following April, keen as ever, his remaining eye as keen and straight as in the old days, but he was made second in command, and never joined the squadron again. "C" Squadron was never the same after this, although we got a capable leader in his place. A different spirit crept in; little points in the men's bearing or dress began to be neglected in favour of the idiosyncrasies of our new commander. Our new skipper was a brave and capable man, but he was of a type quite different from Stephens.

We arrived at Flesquières about midnight, and got some sleep in some dug-outs there. Early next morning the heavy bombardment increased to great intensity, and about 9 a.m. we heard that the Boches had broken through and were coming on.

No one knew quite what was going to happen to us. Some thought that most probably we should be brought up to counterattack. In the ordinary course our horses were to have come up and the division was to have been reformed mounted. Our horses arrived and orders for the division to reform as soon as possible at Fins. The German attack had been on a wide front and had stretched from Moeuvres on our left as far as Epehy. Gouzeaucourt had been captured and the Huns were now west of it.

Our brigade galloped up to the ridge just west of Gouzeaucourt in the afternoon, but the Boches had been held and there was no fear of their breaking through.

On our right an Indian Cavalry Brigade had been in action in Pigeon Ravine near Epehy. Oddly enough this was where Brigade H.Q. had been when we held the line during the summer. In most places the attack was repulsed, but in some the Huns were successful. Next day, December 1st, I was sent out to reconnoitre the way to Quentin Mill on the ridge the other side of Gouzeaucourt, in case we should be required there. The ground over which the attack had taken place was a quaint sight. It was strewn with dead of both sides, bits of equipment, British and German machine-guns, rifles, helmets, etc.

From the Gouzeaucourt ridge there was a fine view for miles to the east, and I could distinctly see the flashes of the German guns in action, and even German transport on the roads. That afternoon I happened to meet a master from my old school, who had taught me History for many terms. It is astonishing how you come across people like that.

This finished the Battle of Cambrai for us. It had been another disappointment for the cavalry, though on the whole it was a success. We stayed at Fins a few more days in the same bivouac. The Huns now switched a couple of long-range guns on to our valley, which fired intermittently for several days. Our cook thought the shells were aeroplane bombs, and for a long time declared it impossible to light a fire to cook without drawing more bombs.

On December 8th we left for billets and settled down for Christmas just south of Amiens. I was not sorry to leave that district. The infantryman when he has to remain in a bleak place can usually find himself some kind of cover, and can keep warm, since he has only to come out to eat and wash, etc., but the cavalryman has to be out at all hours, feeding and grooming horses, cleaning saddlery, etc. I believe that his is the hardest lot. Think what it means to go into a field in the rain and pitch dark, and have to picket down horses; think of the packs and saddles, etc., in the mud, when there is nothing to hang them on to. Lucky is the man who only has himself to look after.

CHAPTER 16

Christmas Festivities

We fully expected to spend Christmas in our new billets; but we had not been back from Cambrai more than a week before we had to send another trench party up to the line near Hargicourt. On this occasion I was left with the horses, so that I had a fairly comfortable time, but I was sorry that we were not to eat our Christmas dinner all together.

The preparations for this feast are always most elaborate. You have to scrounge round for turkeys, geese, ducks, chickens, rabbits, pigs, guinea-fowls, and anything you can get hold of. It is very hard to get enough turkeys to go round, but the others make excellent substitutes. Of course, all the above are only to be had at exorbitant prices, but regimental funds usually come to the rescue with a fairly generous subscription. It needs, however, a lot of stuff to provide a dinner for a hundred British cavalrymen, and a good deal has to be paid for by the officers.

On this occasion we had a plum-pudding ration. The way this was supplied was wonderful; it takes a good deal of organisation to provide an army of several millions.

The troop mess-rooms are usually decorated with holly or some substitute, and sometimes home-made Chinese lanterns can be had.

It is the custom for the squadron leader to come round the Christmas dinners and make a short and humorous speech to each troop. Any remark which has any pretence to being at all funny is of course greeted with roars and cheers, since everyone is in the best of spirits.

On more than one occasion I have had to address my own troop in the absence of the squadron leader. Each time I expressed the hope that we should eat our next Christmas dinners on the Rhine; and my prophecy of 1917 was not far wrong.

In the evening we usually had a concert. Now in every body of men there are always some comedians and musicians. Our squadron was no exception, for we had a good deal of talent. We had two first-rate "Jews," who used to "argue the point" about money matters; also, a couple of Pierrots who blacked their faces, dressed up in the most grotesque clothes and sang to a guitar accompaniment. I think these were our star performers.

Our cycle orderly made a capital girl—I think anyone could have fallen in love with her—and Sergeant Coates used to conduct what he called a Hungarian band, dressed up in Hun caps, etc. He used to issue orders in some sort of German at the top of his voice, and march them up and down as though they were on the square. My servant was a member of this band and no mean performer. On one occasion he gave "lip" to the bandmaster, who flew at him with such truly Prussian frightfulness that he had a lump on his head for quite a week afterwards.

Besides the humourists there were also men who sang the most sentimental songs. All soldiers seem to know and like such songs as "Come Sing to Me," "Love's Garden of Roses," "God Send You Back to Me," etc. You often hear them singing these when cleaning their saddles and at the most extraordinary times. Our squadron sergeant-major used to stage manage these concerts; he maintained a rigid discipline amongst the spectators; when he got up on the stage to announce the next item, you could have heard a pin drop. Anyone who was at all rowdy he froze with an icy look, and a second offence was usually punished by forcible ejectment from the hall. He was a man of enormous personality and a really fine soldier.

The sergeant-major in a squadron is about the most important person in it. He is responsible for the discipline and the conduct of the N.C.Os., just as the squadron leader is for that of the officers. No one can be a successful S.S.M. without possessing tremendous strength of character. Ours certainly had it, and was far the best in the regiment, if not in the brigade.

I suppose that not many people outside the army know that all owners of common names have a nickname. For instance, all Smiths are "Gunboat," all Lees "Bodger" or "Jigger," and all Murphys are "Spud." All Scotchmen, of course, are "Jock." This tends sometimes to lead to confusion, since in one troop in the squadron there were no less than three of these. Most of the horses seem to have names, too, for the men get extraordinarily fond of them when they have had them any time. I think the commonest names are Bob, Bill, Kitty and Kate. I have known some called Herbert, and even Parson, Cuthbert and Leonard. Also various times I have heard animals called Charlie Chaplin, Champagne-Charlie, The Bullock, Ox-Tail, and the most absurd names.

The men are fearfully sensitive about a horse they have had for long. I once saw a man actually burst into tears because we had to throw his horse to clip it. This is a spirit to encourage, because the fonder a man is of his horse, the better he will look after it. After the Battle of Arras, a lot of horses collapsed and almost all their owners sat up all night with them, in many cases by the roadside, giving them morsels to eat and where possible a hot drink. Sergeant Coates saved his mare in this way. He had had her during the whole war, and was very much attached to her. She recovered and did another fifteen months' service before she was killed during the battle of August 8th, 1918.

When a trench party is away, it naturally means that the men left behind have four or more horses to look after, and the officers, too, must do some grooming. To look after so great a number is very hard work. There is great danger sometimes of the men becoming "fed up" and depressed, a state of mind which often leads to crime. An officer occasionally has very difficult cases to deal with. I will recount one which came before me. Corporal James who was about my best section leader, a first-rate tactician and map-reader, and splendid at looking after men and horses, was late for roll-call one evening, and when reproved answered

Sergeant Coates back; the natural result was arrest.

Now Corporal James had been out in France over three years, had gained the Military Medal and was, I should say, the best corporal in the regiment. Theoretically, I suppose, he should have had a court-martial and been reduced to the rank of private. But in this case, I argued, who was to take his place? I had not a single man who was capable of doing his job half as well as himself, and his loss was most undesirable. Of course, I saw perfectly well what had happened. He had been making merry somewhere in an innocent kind of way, had forgotten the time and eventually turned up rather excited and too late for roll-call. Now, in the light of common sense, what was to happen to this N.C.O.? You had to remember that it is human to err, that this was the man's first crime since he had been in the Service, and that he had a perfectly splendid record. On the other hand, he had answered back a superior officer—fortunately not in the presence of the whole troop—a serious offence.

What you have to decide in a case like this is whether your command will benefit more by the summary reduction of the man or by his retention in his present rank. In this case I decided on the latter, since to my mind there was no doubt. I therefore dealt with the case myself instead of letting it go before the squadron leader or the colonel, and I believe that most people would have done the same in similar circumstances. I, however, had the man brought before me and gave him such a telling off quietly that I honestly believed that there would be no more trouble with him. I could see he was furious with himself for having lost control of his tongue.

I believed that my way was the right way to deal with this case, and I am now certain of it, for Corporal James is now a squadron quartermaster-sergeant-major, and one of the smartest and best N.C.Os. in the regiment. No one, however, except he himself and I know of this affair, for Sergeant Coates has since been killed.

It is in view of cases like this that I maintain that it is so important for troops to be run by the officers and not entirely by the troop sergeant, as one sometimes sees. In this case, with an apathetic troop leader, Corporal James would have gone before the colonel or a court-martial and been reduced. The result would have been the loss of a first-rate N.C.O., and he would now be a private.

Later I had another very interesting affair to put right. Owing to Corporal Hunter being wounded I had to find another man to take his place. Now it is not easy to find men who are suitable for promotion. To begin with, in war-time, a corporal, lives with his section entirely, and he must have a great personality to be the real leader of it. If you choose an unsuitable man there will soon be a row, and although technically you may fix the blame on to the criminal, yet the real fault is yours for making an unsuitable N.C.O.

Now there was one man in my troop who had the personality and all the other qualities which go to make a good leader of men, but he did not wish to be promoted. The reason was a complicated one and I will explain it here, since it gives an insight into the man's character.

Some time ago Goodheart, for this was his name, had been a corporal in another troop. His section leader there had been corporal, now Sergeant Hine. Now it appeared that Goodheart had also been Hotchkiss corporal in his old troop and, although he had done well, he had never liked the job. He asked his troop leader several times whether he could be taken off it, but was told "No." Even Stephens had ruled that he was to continue being Hotchkiss corporal. The natural thing had then happened. After he had run the Hotchkiss section for almost a year very well, he asked once more whether he could be relieved of the job, but the answer was again "No."

After this, Corporal Goodheart deliberately committed a crime in order to get himself reduced.

Another factor in this case was that Sergeant Hine, who had once been his section leader, was now troop sergeant. Now these two had never been able to get on well together. Corporal Goodheart was extremely conscientious and very sensitive, while Sergeant Hine, although a fine soldier in many ways, was rather hard to get on with. For some reason he had his knife into Corporal Goodheart, and never did anything to help him at all.

Now I saw at once that it was out of the question to have Goodheart a corporal while Sergeant Hine was troop sergeant. I never even asked Goodheart to take promotion, for to begin with I knew he would not accept it, and, secondly, I would not have taken it myself under those circumstances, nor would it really have been fair to ask him. But there came a time when Sergeant Hine was in hospital in England, and of his absence I took advantage to ask Goodheart to become a corporal again. I therefore called him aside one morning and told him that I wanted to promote him.

"Well, sir," he said, "I would rather not."

"Why?" I asked.

"It would be very difficult for me to explain to you, sir," he replied, "but I know I should get into trouble."

"In what way?"

"To begin with, sir, I have never been able to get on with Sergeant Hine. He had his knife into me when we were in another troop, and he dislikes me now. I don't know why, I am sure. But I know that I can never get on with him as a corporal, and that he would lay wait for me and run me in on the first possible occasion. Otherwise I should like to be a corporal again."

"I have heard of this," I said, "but now seems to me an excellent opportunity for you to get promoted. Sergeant Hine is not likely to come back for several weeks."

"I know, sir," he answered, "that I could lead a section perfectly well when Sergeant Hine is not here, but I am afraid he will come back."

"If he does, and you cannot get on, I will get permission for you to revert at your own request."

He was on the point of saying yes, when something stopped him.

"I know what you are thinking of," I continued. "You have never quite forgotten not being allowed to be relieved from your post of Hotchkiss corporal, have you?"

"Well, sir, I did think it a little hard."

"Anyhow," I went on, "if you do accept promotion, I promise you that if you wish to revert at any time, I will allow you. You know as well as I that you have the ability and the personality, and I think it will be a great pity if you remain a private. A man of your character ought to be higher up, oughtn't he?"

He admitted that I was right.

After this he accepted and led his section admirably. He seemed a totally different man from the Goodheart I had known as a private. Then he had been sulky and distrustful. I knew at once that there was something on his mind. I am not ashamed to confess that I was perfectly delighted at having made an ally of this man instead of allowing him to remain with a grievance.

Everything went capitally until Sergeant Hine came back about two months after Corporal Goodheart's promotion. Of course, I knew exactly what would happen. Sergeant Hine immediately began to "get at" the unfortunate Goodheart. I therefore decided to tell Sergeant Hine how matters stood.

"I have never had my knife into him, sir," he said.

"Possibly not, but I think you have not always tried to make things easy for him, have you?"

"He's a man, sir, what always thinks he's right."

"Anyway," I said, "he has done extraordinary good work both in action and in billets, lately, and I have never had a better section leader. Fair play is all that is required: if you will help him, he will help you, but if you do not, he will want to revert."

After this I hoped that things would go better. I called Corporal Goodheart aside one day and asked him how he was getting on.

"Splendidly, sir, so far, but I shall never be able to work well under Sergeant Hine."

"Can't you hit it off, even now?"

"I am afraid not, sir. I think I had better revert. You see, sir, I know very well that when you came to the troop Sergeant Hine and all the officers gave me a very bad character."

"Well, even if they did," I said, "do you suppose that I believe everything I hear? I have not been a soldier long, but I have learned to guard against that. I don't mind telling you that, in the first few days that I was in the troop with you, I saw that there was something wrong with you. And I am now out to remedy it. I think you will find that you will get on better now. You will have to try for another week and see how things work?"

"Yes, sir, if you really wish me to."

"I certainly do, and I shall do everything in my power to help you. If you cannot get on you may revert in accordance with my promise."

"Thank you very much, sir."

Since then things have gone well, and I shall be very surprised if Corporal Goodheart is not a sergeant on demobilisation. If this man becomes a sergeant and eventually a warrant officer, I shall look upon the whole affair as a great diplomatic success: moreover, it will give me great personal satisfaction. After all, more than the least pleasure in the world is to be got from doing a good turn to one's subordinates.

From our billets we used often to go into Amiens buying various stores for the squadron or the mess. We got to know the old town pretty well, especially the restaurants such as the Cathedral, the Godbert and Les Huîtres.

I have pleasant recollections of many pleasant luncheons and dinners there. Amiens was like a kind of club: I used to meet all kinds of unexpected people whom I had not seen for years. About the end of January, I went up to the trench party for a few days, but the division came out during the first week in February. We arrived at Saleux Station one very cold afternoon. Horses met us to convey us to billets. Now these horses had not had a great deal of exercise, and the journey back was one of the most amusing I have ever known.

Most of the brutes kicked and bucked hard for the first mile, and not a few men were unseated, which was not surprising since they had not ridden for six weeks. My own mare was particularly troublesome, and I very nearly managed to repeat my

Sandhurst performance. Neame, my groom, who had a sense of humour, has never forgotten that ride; nor have I.

On February 8th we moved up to St. Christ, near Péronne, to relieve an Indian Division who were going to Egypt.

St. Christ is right in the middle of the devastated area of the Somme: there is not a house or an inhabitant for miles. We marched *via* Boves, Harbonnieres, and the main Amiens-St. Quentin road, completing the journey in two days.

St. Christ is a dismal looking place, but was not at all uncomfortable. The horses were all in good sheds, and the men in huts and dug-outs. The officers' quarters were very nice; we had a regimental mess instead of the usual squadron messes, and this did a lot of good. I have explained that we often saw but little of other squadrons, so that the three weeks during which we were there all together did a lot to strengthen esprit de regiment.

About the middle of February, we began to hear a lot of talk about a German offensive. All kinds of opinions were expressed by both officers and men; most people seemed to pooh-pooh the idea. One day, however, a pamphlet came round from Army H.Q. explaining that owing to the Russian collapse the enemy had a large number of divisions in reserve on the western front, and would probably use them in one last desperate blow for Paris and the Channel ports. This had to be read to all ranks. The next thing that happened was that one regiment of each brigade in the division was kept saddled up ready to move at a few minutes' notice between dawn and dusk. However, this was only kept up for about ten days, after which we sent up another dismounted party to the line near Maissemy and Pontruet, just north of St. Quentin.

Nothing exciting happened here, and we were relieved on March 13th by the 24th Division. On March 15th, I think, the powers that be had decided that the German offensive was imminent, and accordingly our three cavalry divisions were placed in reserve, one to each corps, on the threatened sector. Our division was sent down *via* Ham and Guiscard to Grandru, where we bivouacked amongst the woods. The weather was ideal and our camp was in a delightful spot.

Grandru lay about ten miles behind the front which passed near La Fère, and northwards ran near Mennesis and up to St. Quentin. Everyone thought that in case of a break-through by the Huns there would be a lively mounted show for us.

The day after we arrived at Grandru we received orders to tell off a dismounted party, which was to be held ready to embus at short notice if required. The party was actually paraded for embusing practice at a selected point and all details were gone into. Everyone was rather disappointed at the thought of an infantry show instead of a cavalry battle, but we had to "lump" it.

Those who had recently come back from the cavalry school at Bussy thought this very odd, for the one doctrine on which most stress had been laid was that whatever the size of your command, and whatever the circumstances, you *must* keep your "mobility" until the last moment. In other words, don't dismount and leave your horses to fight on foot until you are absolutely forced to. Not more than a week after the breaking up of the school we found all these doctrines flung to the winds. I think no one was more annoyed than General Greenly. I know just what he thought; so, did his staff, according to the story, for I was told that he couldn't be approached with safety for several days after he received this order.

The thought in everyone's mind was "Why bother us with horses if we are never to use them?"

CHAPTER 17

The Opening of the German Offensive

On March 19th we received a message that, from prisoners' statements and other indications, our Intelligence thought that the German blow might fall at any moment. The sector of the front behind which we were situated was stated as being on the front of attack. We therefore had plenty of warning. The Germans had made no secret of their intended drive, indeed, they had advertised it in many ways. One prisoner said that there was to be a bombardment of several hours, chiefly with gas shell, and that afterwards the infantry and artillery were to advance in line together.

At about midnight on the night of March 20/21st the bombardment opened, and it was a bombardment too: the whole sky was lit up for miles. Everyone got up to see the show.

At about 3 a.m. we got the gas alarm, but no gas arrived, though I was told that our interpreter sat with his mask on for hours. I rather think, however, that this is a good story at his expense. The bombardment was continued until about 5 a.m., when it died away. We guessed that the attack was probably timed for that hour. During the morning bad news came in. The Germans had broken our outpost and second lines and were still advancing.

About 12 noon the dismounted party was ordered out and embussed without a hitch. As they marched away, we could not help thinking what a pity it was that 200 highly trained cavalry-men should have to go into action on foot. To begin with our kit is no use for mobile warfare dismounted. A man cannot carry blankets and all kinds of paraphernalia unless he has an equipment specially designed for this kind of thing. I think a regiment of cavalry marching into action on foot is a most depressing sight. Give our men a horse and arms and they will do anything and go anywhere, but to send them off on foot is to crush the cavalry spirit out of them.

What of the lessons which we learnt at Bussy,
Oh, ye who sent our men on foot to Jussy?

Just previous to this I had again to take over the job of adjutant as Hopkins was sick. As on this occasion I held the job for five months I got the acting rank of captain, which is always nice, though I do not like adjutant's work. In billets there is too much sitting indoors for my taste, and besides, you have no show of your own to run, but are simply the tool of everyone else. However, there was no one else who was trained for the job, so I had to do it.

Our Brigade Headquarters had gone up with the dismounted party, and I had to act as staff-captain for two days. I did not enjoy this, as everything was hurry and bustle, and preparations were being made to clear away all surplus stores and material in case of a real breakthrough by the Germans. The telephone from the division hardly ceased ringing while I was there; first it was rations, then water troughs, then reinforcement for the dismounted party, then the formation of a mounted party, and goodness knows what. By the end I was almost as short-tempered as the A.A.Q.M.G. at the other end of the phone.

As the day wore on (the 22nd) the news was still worse and it became evident that we should have to move the horses, as the Boche was only seven miles away. About midday we received an order to send up a troop of thirty men under an officer, to fight mounted. As soon as the authorities saw that it was going to be real open warfare, there was at once a cry for mounted men.

The infantry were saying, "Where is the cavalry? Never there when wanted," etc. It was true: we were not there as cavalry, for all our men were heavily engaged on their flat feet near Jussy and Mennesis.

On the 23rd we received orders to saddle up and march. You can imagine what this meant. We had about six horses to each man, so it took something like three hours to saddle up. Eventually we left, and a fine sight we must have looked. The colonel was leading three horses, and all the officers three, four or five. To make matters worse, all the roads were crammed with transport and traffic of all kinds.

We were only just away in time, for that evening the Huns got into the woods just above Grandru, and the next day were past the village itself.

We marched that evening to Pontoise, where we bivouacked for the night. Now it is no joke for one man to off-saddle six horses, especially in the dark; on the way we roped in a labour company and got them to help. It was amusing to see these fellows, many of whom had never handled a horse before, trying to off-saddle and saddle up. Very few of them knew which end of a horse was his bows and which his stern. Some even tried to off-saddle without undoing the girths, and were trying for all they were worth to slide the saddles over the horses' quarters. However, those labour men, many of whom were very elderly, did very useful work and I take off my hat to them.

Luckily the weather was fine, so things were not so bad. Our second in command had brought away a couple of barrels of beer and some canteen stores and these were issued that evening. German aeroplanes were very active all night and there was a lot of bombing.

Appilly, which had been our railroad, received special attention.

Our G.S.O.2 paid us a visit during the night, and explained what was going on. The enemy had attacked on a front of something like eighty kilometres, and had used forty fresh divisions on each of the first two days. The rate of advance had slackened, but the enemy were still making progress.

Next day we moved on through Carlepont to Ribecourt, a village fourteen kilometres north of Compiègne. Here we had orders to send seventy led horses to fetch the remnants of the dismounted party back. There were some long faces at the thought that only seventy of our men were left, but this turned out to be a pessimistic estimate, for, although only about fifty got back that day, eventually about 130 returned. The dismounted party had been up to Mennesis where they had some lively fighting, and some very pretty shooting at close range, especially at some of the bridges over the canal which they had swept with Hotchkiss and rifle fire as the Huns tried to come over. They had, of course, had absolutely no sleep and were all dead tired. That night we had to send up another mounted party of thirty men; these had some lively times in the woods near Noyon, and suffered a good many casualties.

That night the whole sky was lit up by the flames from Noyon, which was burning. All the roads were full of inhabitants who were fleeing from the invader, many for the second time during the war. I think this was one of the saddest sights I have seen. Every woman had a cart or wheelbarrow and many had little children or babies in arms. Some had come many miles, and a lot fainted from sheer exhaustion and lay down on the side of the road. We did what we could to help them—our men are wonderful in that way—but there were so many that the stream seemed unending.

A column of British lorries picked up some. I saw whole families with their portable worldly goods being conveyed to Compiègne, in this way. They must have blessed our lorry drivers that day.

On the afternoon of the 25th we reached Compiègne. One felt hopelessly out of it at having to keep on going back and back instead of being able to fight.

We bivouacked that night in the large wood south of the town, and the next day moved to a point about two miles west of it. Here the remnants of our various detachments came back:

the division was reformed at last. I do not know who was the staff officer responsible for this feat, but it certainly was no mean achievement to collect our forces, which had been scattered far and wide over the countryside mounted, on foot, in buses, etc.

Everyone's spirits rose to a high level at the thought that we were at last capable of doing something in our proper capacity.

That afternoon we marched to Moyvillers, where we spent the night and got straightened out a bit: there was hard work before us.

CHAPTER 18

The Defence of Amiens

The news from the front was not encouraging. The enemy was still advancing. In the north he had got Bapaume and was streaming across the old Somme battlefields to Albert. Further south, Péronne had fallen on the first day, and the Huns were miles past Ham and apparently marching fast on Montdidier and Amiens.

Moyvillers is on the Beauvais map, and of these there was only one in the brigade—the general's. At 5 a.m. the next morning, the 27th, a real flurry and bustle started. A report came in that German cavalry had taken Montdidier and were pushing on in the direction of Amiens. Another column was said to be advancing from Noyon.

"B" Squadron was therefore ordered to go as fast as possible to Prouleroy, seize the high ground there and push patrols to Cuvilly and Rollot. This would have been easy with a map, but the unfortunate Thompson had none. How we got there I have never been able to discover; but we found the way somehow. It is never pleasant to be doing anything when someone behind is shoving you on all the time. In this case the rest of the brigade was coming on fast: the whole atmosphere was one of "for heaven's sake get on."

The inhabitants of the villages which we passed had not heard that the Huns were close to them and were fairly calm; but when they saw this force arriving at full gallop, they began to get the "wind up." Many came and said, "For heaven's sake, tell us what is happening," or "Must we leave?" I told them that there was no danger, though no one really knew what was happening.

When we arrived at Prouleroy the brigade halted and patrols were sent forward to find out whether there were any signs of the enemy. None were found, and the whole brigade then advanced to Montgerain. Here we got more information. A column of Boches was reported marching westwards from Montdidier along the Broyes road, and our regiment was ordered to go as fast as possible to Plainville and stop them reaching the railway, which is the main Paris-Amiens line.

We accordingly set off at a great speed *via* Sains-Morainvillers and the wood just north of it. We went in line of troop columns with an advance and a flank guard, but met with no interference. Sains-Morainvillers was absolutely deserted by inhabitants; there was not a sign of life except for a few cattle in the fields, and some poultry. The inhabitants had carried off everything that they possibly could, and now the village was left to await the invader.

We marched on to Plainville, but apart from a few Hun patrols, which were seen coming out of Montdidier, we saw no enemy force. Here we remained until the next day, when news came through of the German bid for Amiens.

We had a comfortable night in Plainville, and men and horses had a much needed rest. When we arose next day, I heard a big commotion going on next to where I was sleeping. It appeared that the colonel's servant had lost his (the colonel's) razor, and that the C.O. was raising Cain about it. A colonel of cavalry is not generally the most sweet-tempered of individuals at four in the morning, and ours was no exception. To make matters worse, no one had had much sleep, and this does not improve one's manners. In the end I had to lend him my razor.

About midday we watered and fed and left for the Amiens front. We marched *via* Chepoix, Quiry-le-Sec, Folleville, and La Faloise to Cottenchy, where we bivouacked. It was 8 p.m. when we arrived and just getting dark. I got little sleep that night for all kinds of orders kept arriving, amongst them being that we should parade at 8 a.m.

We spent the night in a horribly cold barn through which the wind whistled from at least three sides. At 8 a.m. we marched off at a great pace through Le Paraclet, Fouencamps, Thezy, Hailles, and Castel, across the railway line to a point in the valley just east of Thennes. Here we learnt what was happening. The Huns had got Mezières and Villers-aux-Erables, and had got a footing in the Bois de Moreuil. The Canadian Cavalry Brigade, which had spent the night in the Bois de Sencat, was already in action, and our brigade was to help them to retake the wood and to secure the high ground between the wood and the Moreuil-Amiens road.

Accordingly, "C" Squadron was sent off to join the Canadian Brigade. The Huns had got a good way into the wood and a counter-attack was to be launched immediately. To effect the repulse of the enemy, a mounted party was sent round the northern side of the wood, while a dismounted attack was made through the wood itself.

Meanwhile, south of the wood, the remaining two squadrons of our regiment with a squadron of one of the other regiments in the brigade, were sent to gallop up and seize the ridge between the wood and Moreuil village. This was done just in time, for had we been a few minutes later the Boches would have been on it. Luckily, we got there first and were in time to catch a party of Huns in the open trying to come out of the wood to seize the ridge. Our rifle fire was too much for them and they had to stay inside the wood.

But our position was an exposed one; the Boches brought some machine-guns into the edge of the trees and started firing hard. The ground was pasture, but the grass was not long and there was practically no cover. Our second in command was hit in the head: his steel helmet saved his life and the wound amounted only to a deep cut. The dismounted attack through the wood was making good progress and we had some pretty shooting at the retreating Huns. Almost the whole wood was now ours again. About 11 a.m. a battery of French 75s. opened fire on us, apparently mistaking us for Huns. Luckily, they only fired a few shots at the ridge where we were, most of their attention being confined to the northern exit of Moreuil village, which they plastered heavily. It is most unpleasant being shelled by your own artillery: there is quite enough to put up with when the Boche guns are strafing you without drawing the fire of your own.

Our R.H.A. battery did some first-rate work; their shrapnel was beautiful to watch, every burst a few feet off the ground. They scattered several parties of Boches beautifully. Once during the morning, I was sent to the battery with a request to cease firing for a few minutes as we were going to push some troops further out. I shall never forget the face of the subaltern who was shooting the battery when he received this message: it went from the height of joy right down to zero. However, he was able to open fire again in a few minutes.

The casualties so far had not been really heavy. The machine-guns in the wood had caught a few of our men as we galloped up to the ridge, and some horses had been killed, and wounded too. The German artillery was nothing to worry about just then; but about 5 p.m. a heavy bombardment was opened on the wood and its surroundings, and the Huns attacked. They were not, however, able to get a footing in the wood, as it was now strongly held by ourselves and some Canadian cavalry, and the Boches were beaten off leaving a few prisoners in our hands.

About midday the colonel sent me with a message to Brigade Headquarters, which were supposed to be in a corner of the wood to our left rear. I accordingly mounted "Kitty," my mare, and set off accompanied by Neame, my servant. I crossed the ground between me and the wood pretty quickly, as a good many "overshies" were whistling above our heads. After crossing two little dips, I arrived at the edge of the wood and had just turned round the angle of it where I believed Brigade Headquarters to be when I heard Neame shout: "Look out, sir," and I realised that there was indeed need for caution, for instead of our Brigade Headquarters I saw only some thirty-five yards away a group of about a dozen Huns on the edge of the wood. This was the last thing I expected to see here.

I think they must have been as surprised as I was, for they did not fire until I turned and galloped away. I remember that one had lost his steel helmet and I saw that he had light red hair. Just as I turned to gallop off several of them fired together. Their marksmanship must have been very third-rate, for I heard at least two bullets strike the trees above my head. How they missed us at that range I can't think. Eventually I found Brigade H.Q. in another corner of the wood about 500 yards from where I had just come. I explained where I had seen the Boches, and how the position of my own regiment would be very precarious if the Huns came on any further. The general said that they had come in from the left flank and that the squadrons of another regiment had been ordered to counter-attack and regain the lost ground. This was accomplished about 1 p.m. and then I went back to report to the colonel.

About two o'clock it began to rain hard and continued until dark. This made things very unpleasant, as it was very cold also. I had to write several messages for the colonel, and did not find this easy because message-writing in the rain was a fearful job, especially if you had to make several copies of your message. Your carbon paper got ruined and the wind blew it all over the place. Usually you were in a great hurry, which made things worse.

When the Boches were attacking they fired off numbers of flares of various colours as signals to those behind. Personally, I believe that these flares were just as great a help to us as to them, for we were able by this means to discover how far they had got when we could not actually see the Boche troops.

The one thing I dreaded was an attack by German cavalry. Had the Huns brought up a cavalry division and pushed it through, it would have been extremely awkward. The leaders would have suffered severe losses from our fire, and we should have warmed them up in mounted combat as well, but we were holding so large a front that a bold employment of cavalry would have made our position very unpleasant. There was nothing behind us, except a few French territorials. It would have been extremely embarrassing if Boche cavalry had appeared on the scene.

The ground which we had gained was held until the evening, when we were relieved by an infantry battalion. About midnight we returned to Thennes, where we billeted for the night. All the horses were left saddled up, and we were ready to move at once if necessary. Strangely enough we got a big mail that night with the rations. I remember that I received 200 cigarettes, a bill from my tailor, a letter from my mother, and a box of chocolates from some kind aunt.

It is astonishing how you are in the thick of a battle at one moment, and half an hour afterwards you are busy with news from home, and parcels, and wondering what will be the dimensions of your tailor's bill!

That night passed fairly quietly; about 8 a.m. the Huns started plastering Thennes, and a lot of rifle fire came from the wood in front. I suppose the Huns must have attacked again.

We had a good lunch about 11 a.m.; our mess cook was a marvel, although he was always a most disreputable sight and was often cursed into heaps by the colonel. We had hardly finished lunch—in fact I had not—when we got the order to mount, and went at full gallop up the ridge just on the left of where we had been the day before. Our outposts had reported signs of attack. The Huns had opened a pretty heavy shoot on the valley east of Thennes and on the ridge itself. We had a few casualties getting there, including the colonel, who was blown to atoms by a shell which pitched just under his horse.

When we got half-way up the hill, we got the order "action," and doubled up to the top, where we lay down in extended order. The next thing I saw was the finest sight I have ever seen in the war. A long line of grey figures debouched from the wood and started advancing towards us. Machinegun sections on the flanks covered their advance; one of these reached a haystack

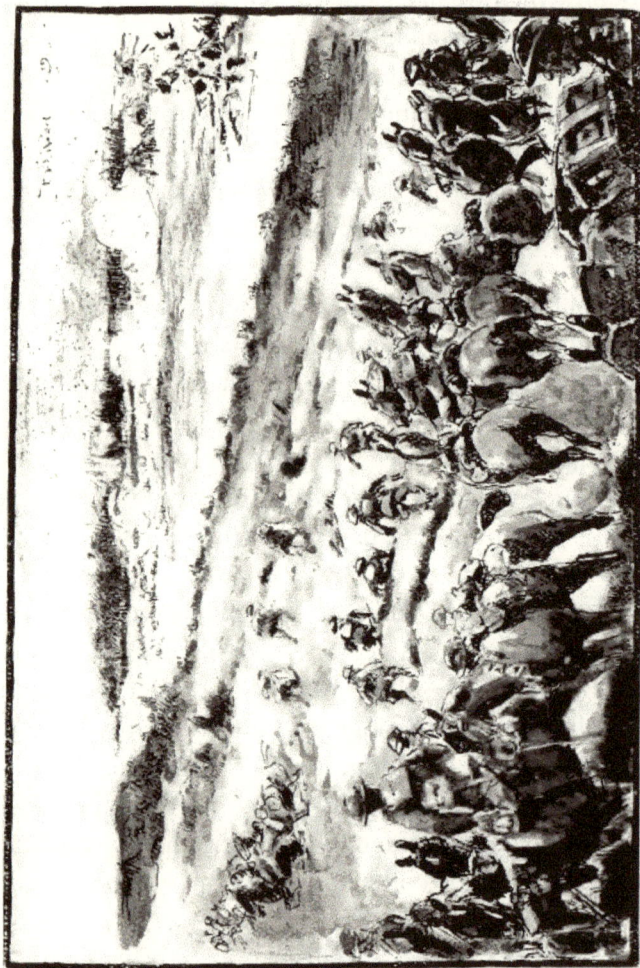

Half-way up the hill, we got the order "action," and doubled up to the top, where we lay down in extended order.

some hundred yards from the wood and from there poured an unpleasant fire into us. About 200 yards behind the line of grey figures, came a second, and behind that a third. I could distinctly make out a Boche officer carrying a pair of field-glasses. The helmets of these Huns showed up remarkably white; I suppose it was the rain on them which made them show up so.

But our men are trained to shoot as well as ride, and shoot well they certainly did on that occasion. The attackers lost very heavily as they crossed this open space. I could see our shrapnel tear great holes in their ranks. They were far too close together for a movement of this kind and tended to "bunch." I suppose they must have come on about 300 yards out of the wood, when they found it too hot for them. First a few of them wavered and lay down. Then the whole front line stopped, and eventually they broke and ran back into the wood. The officer leading the first wave was still untouched. I saw him shake his fist at his men as they retired, but he never went back himself. He stayed where he was until he dropped dead. One couldn't help admiring that fellow. He was a short, stumpy little man and rather fat. The Boche officers may be brutes, but they are no cowards under fire.

Our R.H.A. battery did magnificent work again and seemed to have the range to a nicety. Our friend, the 75th battery of the day before, saw the target also and fired salvos of shrapnel. It was capital seeing the bursts of the shells all in line, and the Boches scattering in all directions.

But the most wonderful sound is that of rifle fire. We had pretty well the whole brigade dismounted there, except for a reserve kept mounted; and, what with our Hotchkiss and machine-guns, it must have been pretty warm where the Boches were. The whole ground outside the wood was strewn thick with dead and wounded Huns,

I had often been told the importance of good fire discipline, and how in action you could hardly hear yourself speak. I couldn't even hear a word that Hunt said. Hunt was now in command.

The attack had been repulsed for the time being, but another was fully expected. When it did come, however, it was rather half-hearted, and was easily repulsed. The German fire had caused us a lot of casualties, especially on the left where most of the shell fire was. We were lying in the open and had no cover at all, since cavalry have no entrenching tools, except those on the packs, and there had not been time to bring these up. Towards three o'clock an infantry battalion came up and reinforced us. They had entrenching tools, and in time all our men had some kind of cover. It was the machine-gun behind the haystack which had caused the most casualties. Eventually we got the guns on to him, and he had to come out like a rabbit out of a hole. I do not think many of that section gained the cover of the wood again.

Things now looked like getting lively on our left. I could see a lot of Huns advancing near Hangard and on the high ground the other side of the valley. We were, however, holding the wood the side of the hill and gave them a pretty warm reception. They eventually took the wood, but the 4th and 5th Cavalry Brigade retook it next day.

The weather was cold and stormy, but there were sunny intervals. We could distinctly see Amiens Cathedral in the distance behind us, with the sun shining on the wet roof. No doubt the Huns saw it too, but they never reached it.

We stayed in our position for three more days, after which we were relieved and went back to Cottenchy. I think everyone was glad of a rest; not least the horses, which had had their saddles on almost continuously for over a week.

CHAPTER 19

Paris-Plage

The total casualties during the battle were four officers killed and five wounded, and a hundred and forty-five other ranks killed and wounded. This amounted to practically half the strength with which we had gone into action. A good many horses had been lost too. We captured two German horses, and these were by no means sweet-tempered animals. They were in good condition, but possessed every conceivable vice—such as wind-sucking, kicking, biting, refusing to leave other horses, etc.

If we were to fight again, we should have to receive a large number of reinforcements both in horses and men. On April 5th we moved to Camon, an eastern suburb of Amiens, where we began to get straightened out. The regiment received as reinforcement a squadron of yeomanry, lock, stock and barrel, and this made us very nearly up to strength again, both in men and horses.

You can imagine the trouble of dividing these out to each squadron, since each wanted to replace certain specialists who had been lost. For instance, one squadron had lost mostly shoeing smiths, another mostly signallers or Hotchkiss personnel. It is a significant fact that every single Hotchkiss team had lost heavily. I suppose the reason is that a Hotchkiss gunner cannot take cover so well as the ordinary man. When he is firing, his head and shoulders are bound to be more exposed than other people's. Another point worth noticing is that three men close together, such as the No. 1 of the gun, the No. 2, and the observer are bound to attract fire.

The observer must be a few feet away from the others. The drawback to this is that, if he is not close to the other two, he cannot make himself heard. My own idea is that for this reason the observer is not necessary. To my mind it is waste of a man. Why not let No. 2, the loader, do the observing? He could do it perfectly well.

On April 6th we marched to Vauchelles near Abbeville, where the reorganisation was continued. Some more reinforcements came up, and, luckily, a few Hotchkiss men. With these we were able to get more or less straight.

The loss and wastage of kit and equipment during a battle is appalling. The dismounted party had lost a lot of theirs, and of the others I don't suppose there was a single man who did not want something replacing. A lot of Hotchkiss guns were useless, hit by shell fire or buried. Serges, breeches, boots, *puttees*, emergency rations, nosebags, water buckets, picketing gear, field-dressings, water-bottles, ammunition, all wanted replacing or replenishing. The drain on our rear services at a time like this must have been very heavy indeed; but the speed with which things came up was astonishing.

On April 9th began the German offensive in Flanders; and we heard that our division was to move up there. This we did, marching *via* St. Riquier, Le Boisle, Hesdin and Fruges to Lynde, a village a few miles from Hazebrouck. I never dreamed that our division would be any use up here as the country is not suitable for cavalry. There are so many dykes and ditches that it is very hard to get off the roads. We never did anything interesting at all. The nearest we got to doing anything was sitting on the slopes of the Mont des Cats being shelled in the rain and the snow. We were kept there as a reserve, but no one ever dreamed that we should be required as cavalry.

April was a vile month as far as the weather was concerned: last year we had gone through the Arras show, and now at precisely the same date the weather was identical with last year's.

While we were up in this district our list of decorations came in. We received four M.C.'s, one D.C.M. and nineteen Military Medals, which was not so bad.

The German offensive in this sector gradually "fizzled" out; the division was gradually withdrawn, and by May 6th, we had settled down in billets near Paris-Plage. Fine weather set in and we soon got the horses more or less in good condition, and the men refitted with clothes, etc. It takes several weeks before you get straight after a show like the one which we had just been through.

Hopkins was now back and I returned to my troop. There were not many of the old ones there now, but luckily, they had been mostly wounded and not killed, and in time several of them returned. Corporal Goodheart and Sergeant Hine had both got the Military Medal.

The first event of interest was a horse strafe: this took place about a month after we had been back from the Mont des Cats. In this strafe many officers of high rank participated, including the brigadier, the divisional commander, and the corps commander, besides hosts of veterinary and remount officials. The first inspection was not a success from our point of view. General Pitman, who held the inspection, placed the horses into two classes—"A." and "B." Very nearly all ours were classed "B."

After the inspection there was a long *pow-wow* of the Olympians to discover the cause of the poor condition of the horses. I do not know what decision was arrived at, but I know perfectly well why the horses were not in good condition. We had been several times to the sands at Paris-Plage and had done a lot of drill and galloping about. It meant seven miles before we got there, and the weather was very hot and the roads dusty. Now no horse will stand much of that on 10 lbs. of oats and 10 lbs. of hay. Besides, they had scarcely had time to recover from the last stunt, in which they had covered something over 300 miles in a few days.

The natural result of the horse strafe was a general strafe in which everyone "copped it" from the brigadier down to the horse himself. The brigadier expressed his displeasure to the colonel, who in turn gingered the squadron leaders. The "hate" then came down on to the heads of the troop leaders, who in turn put the "wind" up the corporals. These abused the private soldiers, and the latter called their horses all conceivable names, most of which are not printable.

This is always what happens when a strafe is begun in high quarters. Down to the rank of squadron leader, all that can be done is to ginger up those below you, but below that a strafe really means something. It means, for instance, a close supervision all round; the troop leader must go out grazing with the thin horses himself instead of letting an N.C.O. do it; he must pay more attention to the way his troop feedman makes out the feeds; he must be eternally going round looking at horses' teeth, and trying to detect minor ailments which may be keeping the horse from putting on condition. He must see every horse watered and fed personally at every feeding time. It is just the same for the section leaders: they must see to like details more closely than before, and the private soldier will be eternally on the move cutting hay for his horse, or doing something more than he did before the strafe.

On this occasion the general ordered the introduction of stock-pots in which were boiled nettles, cabbage leaves, hay seeds, potato-peels, grass, linseed, and every conceivable thing. Reams of paper came round from the division on the care of horses, and it was a pretty busy time.

The inspection itself is rather amusing. Each horse is led past the general while the troop leader stands with him and answers any questions he may like to ask. Now every officer should, of course, know everything about his horses, but this is not always possible. However, as long as you answer something, it doesn't really matter. Personally, I regard these inspections as a time to tell the general of what you are in need, and to speak out. On this occasion he asked me a lot of questions.

"That horse's coat looks bad," he said about one.

"Yes, sir," I replied, "it does."

"What have you done for it?"

"I have asked again and again for salt, which is what it wants, and I can't get it, sir. Is there any chance of getting any? They all want it."

"I will see what I can do."

"Thanks, sir."

"This is a skinny-looking animal."

"It has worms, sir."

"Of course, you have given it worm powders?"

"No, sir, I have not; the vet says he cannot get them. I have several with worms, and they will not put on condition until they are cured."

"H'm. I will see the A.D.V.S. This one looks very poor, too."

"Yes, sir."

"Why don't you cast it?"

"Because it has been out the whole war, and is one of the best horses in my troop, although it looks one of the worst."

"Really, I had no idea it was such a good animal."

Three weeks afterwards he saw me do a practically faultless round in the regimental jumping competition on this horse.

These inspections do a lot of good, although they are a dreadful nuisance. When you know that one is coming off you work like anything to get things right for it. During the strafe which preceded it, and which followed it in an intensified form, my feedman, Snipe, shrank almost to a skeleton. I harangued him for a long time on the subject of the stock-pot, and he hardly left the store where the forage was kept, except to cut nettles, collect the hayseeds and light the stock-pot fire. Everybody spoke in terms of stock-pots; my dreams at night were of stock-pots and chaff, and my second sergeant, who was responsible for the "Q" department, talked of nothing but nose-bags and hay-nets and the quality of the oats, bran and hay. I think he lost a couple of stone, too, while the hate lasted.

The result of all this was miraculous: at the next inspection all my horses were classed "A" except four. The strain had been so great, however, that everyone succumbed to a pyrexia of unknown origin, commonly called P.U.O., which now spread amongst us. This was a most extraordinary disease. I suppose that it was really a kind of flu. It started amongst the men; my servant got it, then I got it, then the other officers got it: everyone had it in turn except one or two. At one time I had only four men left in my troop.

The days we spent at Paris-Plage were really great fun: first of all, we did some regimental drill. This form of soldiering is one long volley of abuse from start to finish. If you walk, you are wrong; if you trot, you are wrong; if you gallop you are bound to be wrong; *ditto* if you stand still. It is really great fun if you have a "hard neck." After this we would do some sword work, and then we used to bathe and take the horses in with us. Some of the horses did not like the sea, but they got used to it all right. After lunch we had sports, such as sack races, etc., and rode back in the evening. Most of the men enjoyed it, but it made a very long day.

We used occasionally to come and dine in Paris-Plage where there were some good restaurants, and nice, hospitable inhabitants whom we got to know. There was tennis to be had at the clubs, and this attracted a lot of people, but, for my part, I preferred cricket. There was a fine ground near the golf links where we had some capital matches. Our division beat the Étaples base team, who had quite a reasonable side, including some county players.

One of our most entertaining forms of amusement was rounders, which we played every evening after dinner. There was inter-troop matches, officers *v.* sergeants, inter-squadron matches and all kinds of contests. The inter-troop games were the most amusing. Topham's servant was the star performer. His place was wicket-keeper. Everyone knows that, in rounders, if the batsman misses the ball three times he has to run.

This was where Jameson came in, he had arms as big as most people's legs and threw with such force that many batsmen preferred to be out than to run the risk of being hit by these Herculean throws. A tennis ball is not very heavy, but a good many preferred not to risk it. If, by any chance, anyone saw that Jameson was going to throw at them, they used to run with a speed which they did not show often.

I once saw Jameson catch two men at the same "base." One ran back but collided with Smith, who was for some reason making for this base also. Just as Jameson "let fly" the two who had collided collapsed in a heap; the ball whistled just over their heads and caught one of the fieldsmen absolutely straight amidships. A rounder was scored amidst cheers, as the fieldsman was incapable of throwing in, and incidentally he had to be excused duty next day and had a bruise on him which looked just as if he had been hit by a hammer.

We had a lot of cricket, and used to take tea out to the ground and make a regular picnic of it as usual. These were some of the happiest days I have ever spent.

A certain amount of training went on, chiefly staff rides for officers or N.C.Os. During one, in which I was instructing my section leaders, the brigadier paid us a visit and asked the situation. I told him and he then asked each corporal several questions, putting to each a different situation. I think the men like being spoken to by a general: everybody does; it makes you feel that he is taking an interest in your doings. They answered his questions fairly intelligently. After he had finished, I ventured to ask the general his views.

"What would you do, sir, in such a case?" I asked.

He said he would do just what Corporal Greatorex would have done, though he did not agree with Corporal Goodheart's solution, and gave a lucid explanation of his reasons. He certainly understood the views of the lower ranks and appreciated their minds. He used to ginger up his staff and his immediate subordinates, but he was a great friend to subalterns and also to the rank and file. Everyone liked him.

While we were in this area there were a number of air-raids on Étaples and Boulogne. The raiders used to pass right over our horse lines *en route* and on the way back. Occasionally they dropped a few bombs on the way, notably on August 1st when they demolished a couple of houses and killed a few of our horses. The inhabitants were in a pitiable state, since they were not used to this kind of thing. A panic-stricken woman is a fearful thing, especially if she has a child in her arms. This raid drove the whole village pretty nearly mad. It was their first taste of war.

On August 1st and 2nd we were preparing for some squadron sports which were to have taken place on August 8th and 9th. However, on those days we took part in a very different kind of sport, as I shall recount in the next chapter.

CHAPTER 20

The British Offensive East of Amiens

Ever since the German thrust at Amiens the town had been under fire of the enemy's guns, which were firing at a range of only fifteen kilometres. This led to the evacuation of the civil inhabitants, and the gay Amiens, with its brilliantly lit restaurants and smart shops, which we had known a month before, became a dull and deserted town. It was primarily for the relief of this place that the battle of August 8th and 9th was fought. The repulse of the enemy, even a few kilometres, would have the effect of freeing Amiens itself and also the railway lines, of which it is a junction.

On August 3rd the division was still round Étaples. We had heard nothing of a move and did not expect one. During dinner that evening we heard the first news of it. No one, however, knew where we were going or what the idea was. We were to march the next evening.

On the afternoon of August 5th everything was got ready, and I was sent off with a billeting party to Maintenay, which was to be our first halt. I was not able to do the billeting until dusk, and most of it was actually done in the dark. Billeting in daylight is hard enough, but by night it is ten times harder. I blessed my Orilux lamp, which was absolutely invaluable. It was a long wait until 2 a.m., when the regiment was due to arrive, but I passed the time in chatting with the mayor, who was remarkably hospitable and gave me and my billeting party a good meal.

About 2 a.m. the regiment arrived and got into billets without difficulty, although there was a pretty good box-up at the watering-place in the dark. The billets were not bad, and I think everyone was fairly comfortable. Luckily, it was fine.

Next night the march was continued to Neuilly L'Hôpital; it poured with rain and was a miserable march altogether. Most people were pretty bad-tempered when they came in, including the colonel, who could not find any of the billeting party, except me. All the others were asleep. Anyway, I had our squadron in billets, and the horses watered and fed, while the others were still standing out in the road.

There was something slightly humorous in knowing that the colonel and all the bigwigs were raving and stamping about the village hunting for their billeters while our men were actually asleep. I have explained that colonels are never very nice-tempered; and you can imagine the effect of being kept waiting for an hour in the rain at 2 a.m. People are not at their best at that hour.

Next morning the colonel explained the scheme. It was the usual kind of thing: infantry was to attack, and if certain objectives were gained our three cavalry divisions were going through to seize objectives further on. That evening we marched to Picquigny, a village about seven miles north-west of Amiens. The attack was to be opened at dawn on August 8th. During the night of August 7/8th Amiens was full of troops going up for the attack. A stream of well over a hundred buses was followed by long columns of cavalry and infantry. We passed through Amiens about 3 a.m.

It was a peculiar feeling passing through the great *boulevards* of that town: not a light was to be seen, and not a soul in the streets except the unending columns of troops. Our division was in support on the 8th, and was not to be brought up until the 1st and 3rd Divisions had got on a bit. We passed out of the town to Longeau, where Cavalry Corps Headquarters were, and turned off to Glisy just as day was breaking.

At 4.20 our bombardment opened. The wind was in the west, and one hardly heard the guns, but the gun flashes and the coloured lights were a wonderful sight. The bombardment was short and sharp, after which our men went over and easily captured the German first lines on the whole front of the attack. The left flank of the attack was somewhere near Albert, and the right, so far as we were concerned, was on the Amiens-Roye road. South of this the French took on through Moreuil and southwards.

After watering and feeding at Glisy we advanced to Hangard Wood, and then again to just north of Aubercourt to the valley south of Marcelcave. The news was good. The 3rd and 1st Cavalry Divisions had gone through, and a large number of prisoners and guns had been captured. I hardly heard a Boche shell all day. I saw a fair number of German dead, but very few of ours. The Boche had been completely surprised and had left everything just as it was. Dug-outs, trenches, shelters, guns—all bore witness to the haste in which the Boches had departed.

About 6 o'clock we got to Caix; our leading troops had got just east of the village. Here we waited for some time and off-saddled. The Huns coughed up a few 5.9s, but nothing to cause much alarm. Some of our officers found a dug-out, where they had some cocoa made, but unluckily I did not know where this was. While I was looking round, the colonel came out and gave the order to saddle up and follow him. I told him that I did not know where Topham was, so he told me to bring the squadron along myself. It was now dark.

After we had gone about a mile Topham caught up, somewhat perturbed at not being told that the regiment was moving off, and I came in for much damning and cursing.

It turned out that we were going to spend the night in a wood just north-west of Caix and were going to relieve the 3rd Division next day. At some cross tracks the 2nd troop lost touch in the dark and got mixed up with some other regiment who were crossing us. It was only after they had gone about a mile out of the way that we discovered that they were lost, and there were cries of "Where is the 2nd troop?" and someone was sent off to find them. After much cursing they rejoined. The crush on those tracks was appalling: guns, transport, infantry, cavalry, and goodness knows what. No one who has never been lost in the dark with a lot of men and horses behind him can know what it feels like. It is worse still if you don't know where you have to go to.

Soon after this we were shown the part of the wood in which to bivouac. I was given two trees, and told to put up a line between them. The wood was full of old German telephone wires, and these became entangled with the horses' feet and caused a lot of delay. We had not nearly enough room and were, in fact, packed like tinned herrings. The 2nd troop tried to make out that I was on their tree, but eventually we got straightened out and had a good night's rest. It was lovely weather, so that it was quite pleasant sleeping in the open.

At dawn next day we paraded. "C" Squadron was to get to the wood south-east of Caix and reconnoitre the enemy's position. My troop was to do advance guard. I moved off in front of the others and passed rapidly through Caix village and out into the open. I directed Corporal Dixon's patrol round one side of it and Corporal Goodheart's on the other. I saw these get well round it and I then galloped up with the other two sections. The two leading sections had got into the wood all right, but had met with a lively fire from the ground east of it. The Huns had a line of rifle-pits about 500 yards farther on. There was no wire there. This information was sent back to the squadron, who came up into a hollow behind the wood.

Here we received orders to remain for the present. Guns were being brought up and the attack was to be renewed at 12 noon. Everything was fairly quiet except for some desultory sniping and an occasional shell which the Huns put over into Caix. Our little hollow behind the wood was very snug, and here we had some breakfast. I have never enjoyed fried bacon more than I did that morning; a fried ration biscuit is a dainty morsel too.

About ten o'clock the Huns began to fire on the wood with a 5.9 howitzer; all the shells pitched in exactly the same place just short of us. I have often wondered why the Huns fire in this manner. Had they searched the whole wood they must have hit us. About eleven o'clock the firing became more lively. A field gun battery and some more howitzers joined in, and a regular barrage was put on the eastern exits of Caix village and all round our little wood. This fire was extremely accurate and must have been "observed." Later I saw the Boche O.P. in Warvillers wood, and realised what a fine view he had had of the wood where we had been lying.

Both Topham's horses were killed and my own mare slightly wounded; luckily only a few men were hit, but it was obvious that we were going to suffer heavy casualties if we stayed there much longer. I was not sorry when we got the order to mount. The Canadians had attacked again and the whole line was advancing. "B" Squadron were ordered to take up the advance-guard and to seize Warvillers, the next village, as quickly as possible. Warvillers was taken all right, together with some Canadian infantry, but Captain Thompson and another officer of that squadron were severely wounded. Otherwise, however, the casualties were light.

Meanwhile the rest of the brigade was halted in the ravine just outside Caix. On our left was a column of the 1st Division, who were just moving off to take a village about a mile to our left front. It was a nasty spot, that ravine, and it was here that we had all our casualties. The Hun observer in Warvillers Wood had ranged his battery to a nicety, and he kept up an unpleasantly rapid fire on this spot. Stephens, who had returned from England and was now second in command, was badly hit all over the body, and eight other officers killed or wounded.

But the greatest carnage was amongst the horses: every shell seemed to knock on to some. My mare (which had been previously wounded) was killed, and every troop suffered a good deal. I had ridden "Kitty" for nearly three years, and was naturally very cut up at her loss. I was only thankful that she died an instantaneous death. I saw one shell land right in the middle of some Brigade Headquarters, and the staff-captain was killed instantly.

Once Warvillers was taken, the shelling became more wild and did us little harm. I had visions of the Boche observer "legging it" out of his O.P. However, he had done his work.

The capture of Vrely was particularly dramatic: there were Boche machine-guns in the village, and they waited until the attackers were close up to them before they opened fire. However, they waited a little too long, for although the losses at such a short range were considerable, a hundred yards does not take long to cover on a horse, and we were soon established in the village.

Just as we left Caix a squadron of about twelve or more German aeroplanes came over. All these had red noses and looked very fine in the sun. They fired a few shots at the mass of cavalry which they saw below them, but apparently either did not dare to come down low and fire at us at close quarters or else thought it *infra dig* to take on anything except other aeroplanes. I suppose that this must have been some "spot" squadron, for I have seen very few Hun planes painted red.

About one o'clock the rest of the brigade moved at a rapid rate over to Warvillers, and "B" Squadron was ordered to try and get Rouvroy, the next village. In this they were also successful, but the Boche resistance was now really beginning to stiffen; we were on the edge of the old battlefields of 1916, and even at Warvillers there were some old trenches. The brigadier wished to take the whole brigade on to Rouvroy, but when we appeared in the open such a hail of machine-gun fire met us that he decided to hold it only with the one squadron already there. Most of the firing came from our left, where apparently the advance had been held up earlier than ours.

The advance from Caix was a fine sight. The country was very flat, and once when I looked round I saw the whole plain behind us black with cavalry. I had never seen 5000 horsemen together before, and I don't suppose I ever shall again.

The day was, however, really rather disappointing: the success gained had not been anything like as great as that of the day before and the casualties far heavier. But it is always the same. The

THE PLAIN BEHIND WAS BLACK WITH CAVALRY

first day is always the best. The important element is surprise, and we had not this in our favour any longer. That night we held on to the ground which we had gained without incident, except that a Hun plane dropped a few bombs about the country just behind Warvillers, and one had the luck to land right amongst the headquarter horses and another in "A" Squadron. A lot of horses and several men were unluckily killed. It was a strange coincidence that the troop of "A" Squadron which suffered on this occasion was the same as that which had been bombed a few days ago near Paris-Plage.

The next night my own troop received a bomb, and every horse except four was killed or had to be destroyed. The sight of all these poor creatures lying horribly mangled was very unpleasant. I couldn't help thinking of all the horse strafes, and the enormous trouble we had taken. And here was all our work undone in a single night!

Amongst the casualties was "Billy," my tool-pack pony. He was one of the best animals I had. He had been in France for over three years and had seen many parts of the front. He had been at Loos; he had been on the Somme in 1916, and also at Arras, Cambrai, and the first Battle of Amiens; he had been twice wounded. Billy was a tremendous favourite; in billets he was allowed to roam loose during a great part of the day when other horses were tied up in the lines. But although he had enjoyed many privileges which had been denied to other horses, his manners had not been ideal.

In the first place he disliked the company of other horses, and used to lay back his ears and kick and squeal when other animals came near him. He also used to resent being groomed and girthed up. On such occasions his habit was to turn round and attempt to seize with his teeth any outlying parts of the anatomy of his master. Sometimes he accompanied the operation with a dental obligato which made strangers very reluctant to approach him. He was certainly a pony of character.

Owing to the hours that he was allowed loose he used to pay frequent visits to the troop cook-house, where he would get bits of bread, biscuits, Maconochie, bully-beef, and even bacon and jam. These morsels he appeared to relish; he showed no signs of irritability then. No wonder he was the fattest horse in the troop. The tools which he had carried had saved the lives of many men, for every man had dug himself a pit with them, but poor Billy's last hour had struck, and he lay dead amongst the comrades he had served so well.

After this we returned to the valley west of Caix. There was no more chance for cavalry for the present.

To give some idea of the surprise which had been sprung on the Huns on the first day of the attack it will interest people to know that one regiment—I believe it was the 5th Dragoon Guards—captured a railway train full of reinforcements or returning leave men at Guillaucourt. They had no idea that an attack had been opened until they saw themselves surrounded.

Many of the Boche guns had not fired a single shot, so suddenly had our onslaught come upon them. I think the 1st Cavalry Brigade alone captured a thousand prisoners.

For our work in this battle our corps received a good chit from General Rawlinson—an infantry man—which was extremely satisfactory.

Chapter 21

The Great Advance

After a few days' rest in Caix valley we were withdrawn to Auxi-le-Château to refit. The losses in personnel had only been some seventy-five, but the proportion of officers was very high, and the losses in horses very heavy. Here I was fitted out with a new troop of horses. I got mostly bays and was on the whole very well pleased with them, although naturally their standard of training was not up to that of the old lot. On August 23rd we moved up to St. Leger where an attack was in progress, but I never entertained a hope that we should do anything here, since this was the old battleground of 1916. Besides we had the Drocourt-Queant line unbroken in front of us.

One of our troops carried a broom on its tool pack, and near St. Leger I heard a humorous Guardsman say:

"These 'ere blokes are going to make a clean sweep of it, it seems."

However, apart from some patrolling, we were not able to do much.

September was an idle month for us, and it was not until October that we performed again. October found us at Inchy, a small ruined village on the Canal du Nord, some five miles from Cambrai. We had dug ourselves in in the fields, and were quite comfortable in dug-outs and shelters made out of old German material and odds and ends out of the village. Our mess was a dug-out covered with a large piece of roofing iron and was quite comfortable. We had a stove "scrounged" from the village, which gave out a certain amount of heat, but mostly smoke. We had built a bathroom out of timber and old water-troughs, and every man in the squadron was able to have a bath regularly.

On the 18th the German withdrawal from Douai began, and our regiment was sent to work under the VIII Corps, which was commanded by Sir A. Hunter-Weston. We marched at 9 a.m. *via* Baralle, Lecluse and Vitry to Esquerchin, where we had good billets.

That night we heard we were to be attached to the 8th Division and were to operate under it next day. Rosy was in command of the squadron as Topham was away. At eight o'clock that night he was sent for to 8th Division H.Q., where he received orders for the next morning.

The situation roughly was that the enemy was withdrawing fast and that the infantry had lost touch. We were to be employed to keep touch and report on his movements. At 7 a.m. we paraded and marched to Raches, where the 24th Infantry Brigade H.Q. were. Our route was necessarily a roundabout one since every bridge had been destroyed by the Boches in their retirement, and pontoon bridges had only been constructed at certain points. Our orders were to pass through the infantry lines and gain touch with the enemy. It was a pity that we had to go such a long way round before we were able to start operations, as the day was far advanced when we really got under way.

At about 2.30 I got the following order:

"Our infantry patrols are reported about Bouvignies. Take your troop, reconnoitre that village, Court-au-Bois, Ghien, Sars-et-Rosières, and Brillon, and if these are clear, push on until you gain touch. No messages wanted until you gain touch with the enemy. Return at dark to Cattelet, (three miles west of Marchiennes), where you will billet for the night."

This sounded very interesting, but the trouble was that I had only a short afternoon before me and a long way to go. Progress was bound to be slow as every cross-road had been ruined, and every bridge over big and small streams destroyed.

Everything went all right until I got to Bru, a small village about a mile and a half west of Bouvignies. I was advancing to Bouvignies when we were suddenly held up by the stream which runs under the road between the two villages. The bridge was down. This was a nasty jar; however, we had to get across somehow, so I told Neame to try the stream on the north side of the bridge and see whether it was fordable. He had just got his horse's forefeet in the water when the brute began to plunge.

The result was that he sank up to his knees in mud and then plunged and kicked more than ever. Eventually he fell on his side in the bed of the stream, and Neame was pinned underneath with his head only just sticking out of the water. It took five men to get him and his horse out. When he eventually was extricated, and stood on the bank covered with mud and soaked from head to foot, he presented a poor picture of a cavalryman. His breeches were badly torn and one of the sleeves of his serge had been wrenched off as he tried to free his arms. It was obvious that the troop could not get across there.

Two courses lay open to me. One was to cross at another village where the bridge was reported to be intact; and the other was to heap rubble into the stream and try to make a solid bottom. I eventually decided on the latter and we got over all right, but a lot of time had been wasted and there was only another hour and a half of daylight in front of me.

Bouvignies was clear, but I had my doubts as to the other places. I had not seen any of our troops at all, and had no information to guide me.

The area north of Bouvignies was being shelled by a whizz-bang battery, but no shells came into the village. Now when you are not certain of a situation, it is always advisable to move prepared for any eventuality, and so we entered the village with an advance guard out, and swords drawn. Our reception by the civilians was a thing I shall not easily forget. An old man with a white beard, whom I took to be the mayor, advanced towards us at the head of a crowd of about a hundred people. He had in his hand a huge bouquet of white chrysanthemums, which he presented to me. I was not prepared for anything of this kind, nor was my mare, for she shied at the bouquet and very nearly unseated me into the ditch. Sergeant Hine, however, accepted the gift with an expression of almost ludicrous dignity.

I questioned the inhabitants about the movements of our own troops and the enemy's, and got some valuable information. The Huns, I was told, had left about 12 noon, and about 2 o'clock a British infantry patrol of six men had passed through the village. That was all they knew for certain, though they thought that the Boches were still in Brillon and Beuvry. Any question I asked was answered by about a dozen people, all of whom spoke at once. I got very angry, I fear, at not being able to hear what they said, as the noise of their combined answers was very confusing, but eventually I found out what I wanted. Here I decided to send out two patrols; the front on which I had to work was a large one, so that the only way I could get my information was by reconnoitring these places simultaneously.

I therefore halted my troop and detailed the two sections for the job. To Corporal Greatorex I gave the following order:

"Take your section and reconnoitre Court-au-Bois, Ghien, and if clear push on to Petit Brillon and eastwards until you gain touch. Messages to be sent to me at Bouteau, and if I am not there send them to Bouvignies church, where you will rendezvous at dark."

To Corporal Goodheart I gave the following:

"Take your section and reconnoitre Sars-et-Rosières and Brillon, and if clear push on eastwards until touch is gained. Messages to me at Bouteau, and if I am not there send them on to Bouvignies church, where you will rendezvous at dark."

After these patrols had got on their way, I pushed on through the wood to Bouteau. I could hear a lot of machine-gun fire in front, and the Tilloy-Brillon road was being shelled by 77s. After a time Court-au-Bois began to receive attention, also the main Bouvignies-Orchies road, The first news received was from Corporal Greatorex, who had gained touch with the Boches on the railway just east of Ponchelet. I had taken a lot of trouble over teaching my section leaders message writing, so I was gratified to see that his message was clear and concise.

(Facsimile of Corporal Greatorex's message.)

1st	Troop	"C"		Squadron
J.G. 1		19th		
Am	at	PONCHELET		aaa
Village	is	clear	but	enemy
are	holding	the	railway	line
aaa	Am		remaining	in
observation	aaa			

L/Cpl. Greatorex.

4.55 p.m.

J. Greatorex.

Corporal Goodheart had found Sars-et-Rosières clear, but had encountered the enemy in the houses at the north end of Brillon. I received one message from him to this effect, and another later to say that Brillon was clear and that he had reached the easternmost house on the Rue de Rosier road. The enemy was still in Rue de Rosier. From Sars-et-Rosières a fine view could be got from the houses, as the country was very flat.

I made no attempt to use the other two sections: I had got all the information I wanted, and I considered that to use the remainder of the troop would be both foolish and useless. About 5.30 we met at Bouvignies, and here I got more details. There had been no casualties except Corporal Goodheart's horse which had been wounded. He had seen two machine-guns in the northern edge of Brillon, and also a column retiring along the road to Rue de Rosier.

At Bouvignies the inhabitants produced some excellent coffee and even sugar. They gave us of their best. They had been half-starved for four years, but did not hesitate to offer us all they had. You cannot help admiring the spirit of these gallant French people. While the men were having something to eat, I wrote a message to the division.

We had to go round by Sokrie to get across the stream which had held us up, since I was not desirous of crossing the broken-down bridge at Bru in the dark.

When I got back, I heard that Polly, who had been out with another troop on our right, had been killed. We were dreadfully sorry about this, as he had been the life and soul of our mess, and was liked and respected by every officer and man in the regiment.

That evening Rosy and I went to see the brigadier: he seemed pleased with our information, and appeared pleased to have cavalry under him.

The next day no advance was carried out by corps orders, owing, I suppose to the difficulty of getting supplies up over the ruined roads, etc., but on the 21st we marched to Rue de Rosier, and the 2nd and 4th troops were employed to reconnoitre St. Amand and report on the river crossings there. The 2nd troop worked round the north side and the 4th troop round the south. Some machinegun fire was encountered, but the Boches were timid and always withdrew after firing a few shots. The 2nd troop "bagged" a couple of prisoners who waited too long and were charged by the advance section. About 3 p.m. St. Amand was clear, and we held the exits until the arrival of infantry.

My troop did not function that day at all. The most trying thing of the day's work was crossing the stream at Rue de Rosier. The bridge had been blown up, and the bottom was very muddy. It was quite impossible to make a solid bottom with the old bridge material, as I had done two days before at Bru. The whole squadron had to get across, and it took very nearly an hour. A number of men fell into the mud and suffered the same fate as Neame. But the worst part was the horses and especially the packs.

My own tool pack was carried by a very lazy horse, who was not a patch on poor old Billy. Snipe was very abusive to this unfortunate animal and called it all kinds of names. He abused it more than ever when it deliberately lay down in the mud and wallowed in it with the utmost satisfaction. I didn't hear all he said, but I heard him say that it was "an 'orse that would as like as not forget to eat 'is feed next, 'e was so lazy." He also called it "parissewks" and a *cochon*, and various other French names. Snipe always was a bit of a French scholar.

Squadron H.Q. came in for a little shelling that day, but nothing serious, and in the evening, we were withdrawn to Brillon. Here was held the funeral of the unfortunate Polly. All the civilian inhabitants turned up, and there must have been 600 people there besides our men. This took place at six o'clock at night. The village presented a magnificent wreath, and the whole ceremony was most impressive, especially as it took place by moonlight. There is something dreadfully sad about the death of someone who is in the first bloom of youth. Polly was only twenty.

As I have already said, he and I had been at Sandhurst together, in the same "ride" there, and had come in for the same abuse from all the riding instructors. What made it even more sad was the fact that it was within three weeks of the cessation of hostilities.

For the next two days the Germans shelled St. Amand heavily, causing over a hundred casualties to civilians. The mayor ordered the town to be evacuated. This was a dreadful sight: several thousand inhabitants streamed down the Orchies road, each with a cart or wheelbarrow, just as had happened during the German offensive in the spring.

The enemy was now standing on the line of the Escaut Canal, and had flooded the country so that there was no possibility of our doing anything for the present. "B" Squadron had been operating with the 12th Division on our left, and had done much the same kind of work as ourselves. "A" Squadron were not employed until November 8th, when they went up with the 52nd Division. On this day the fighting further south had compelled the Boches to leave their positions at Conde and on the Escaut Canal and retire towards Mons.

On November 10th we moved up to Bernissart, and received

orders to be ready to operate again next day. At dawn on the 11th we moved up to Tertre where Infantry H.Q. was situated, and I was sent off to reconnoitre Ghlin and the Mons-Jurbise road, and if clear I was to go to Maisières, a village just north of Mons on the Brussels road.

Just as I was starting off with my troop, an officer passed in a car and shouted:

"Finish 11 a.m.!"

"What do you mean?" I asked.

"Oh, haven't you heard? Hostilities cease at eleven."

At this I heard various opinions expressed by the men behind me. Some thought that the end of the war was quite past all hope, others seemed pleased, but most of them had on an expression of open-mouthed, blank amazement.

"That is the first I have heard of it," I said.

"It is official enough: here it is in black and white," and he showed me the message.

(Facsimile of message.)

All Units

G.575   11th

Hostilities   will   cease   at   11   a.m. to-day   aaa   Troops   will   stand fast   on   line   then   gained aaa   Usual   military   precautions   aaa

SNOUT
7.15 a.m.

A. H. HOLDER Lt.-Col.

After this he left, and I pushed on. My orders were to reach Maisières by 10 a.m. and stay there until relieved by infantry.

Ghlin was all clear, so was the Mons-Jurbise road. From here we got a glimpse of Mons church in the distance. I halted to write a message to Squadron H.Q. which had come up to Ghlin. At the lodge on the edge of the wood where I halted, an old woman actually produced buns and milk for the whole troop. I

Scale of Miles

R.F. $\frac{1}{250,000}$

(2) ROUGH MAP ABOUT 4 MILES TO 1 INCH

think it was goat's milk, but whatever it was it tasted simply delicious. I had not time to eat my buns but crammed them into my pockets. Most of the men, too, left with their pockets bulging with them. I then had a look at Maisières through my glasses. The village lay about a mile ahead of us in a wooded valley, and I could distinctly see people moving about amongst the houses.

There were no signs of any Boches in the vicinity, so I decided to push on as fast as I could. Sending one section in advance, I waited until they had reached a wood which was about six hundred yards away, and then I followed on with the rest of the troop. So far, we had met with no opposition, and I had just sent off my advanced section towards Maisières village when, as we rounded a corner of the wood, a shot was fired at us from somewhere inside. Incidentally, this was the last shot fired at us in the war.

The sound of it had hardly died away and I had not decided what to do, when there broke out in the wood such a galloping and stamping of hoofs, that I thought there must at least be a squadron of Boches inside. What I saw gave me one of the biggest surprises that I have ever had, although, as a matter of fact, I should have been prepared for it. Through the trees I caught sight of six *Uhlans* galloping in single file down a ride parallel to our line of advance. They were about sixty yards inside the wood on our left hand when I saw them, and I could distinctly see the glint of their steel work in the sun, although I believe that their turn out generally is execrable.

There was only one thing to do, and that was to gallop as hard as we could and try and cut them off as they emerged from the wood. But they had a great advantage over us, for they had only to take the first track to the left away from us, and they were bound to gain several hundred yards on us, since the wood was surrounded by a wire fence which prevented us getting in. For the first two hundred yards we were almost alongside each other; indeed, at one point we were only some twenty yards apart, for the track on which they were ran close up to the edge of the wood. Revolver shots were exchanged, and I thought that

THROUGH THE TREES I CAUGHT SIGHT OF SIX *UHLANS*

we were going to bag the whole lot when their track turned sharp off to the left, thus taking them straight away from us.

There was no track leading into the wood, so that I had the mortification of seeing them disappear. We galloped round to the point where their tracks emerged into the open, and I saw that they had made for a thick forest in front. Here I decided to give up the chase, for I had no intention of leading my command into a possible trap, especially an hour before the Armistice. This is the only occasion on which I had seen German cavalry. From what I saw of their horses, I thought that they were in very bad condition; we could see their ribs as plainly as anything, a fact which gave rise to some caustic remarks from my following. But the whole affair was fearfully disappointing; with a little bit of luck we might have bagged the whole lot.

We were already beyond Maisières where I was to stay, so I left one section out on protection and entered Maisières with the other three. It was 10.10 when we arrived. Our reception was astonishing. There must have been 500 people in the square. They had seen us galloping across the valley outside the village, and had turned out in force to receive us. When I went to look at my outpost section outside the village, I found them surrounded by a similar crowd, and I had to drop on Corporal Greatorex for allowing the crowd to press him so tight that, if the enemy had appeared, he would have been unable to do anything.

There were two English girls in the village who had been there the whole war. One was a governess in a neighbouring *château*, and the other had been at school in Mons, which was about three miles away. You can imagine their joy at seeing some English faces again.

I went to see the mayor of the village and told him the news.

"*La guerre est finie*," I said, "and presumably it will never start again."

This news was announced to the crowd, who cheered vociferously. I shall never forget the scene when the church clock struck eleven. The first chimes we heard came from a distant church in Mons. Then Maisières village church boomed out the hour. Caps

167

"La guerre est finie."

were flung into the air, and many women wept at the thought that at last the curtain had fallen on Armageddon, and that all their four years of suffering was now but a dream of the past.

Some musicians were collected and they played the "*Marseillaise*" and the Belgian National Anthem. They also played "God save the King," but with considerable difficulty.

I had to keep my men apart, for military precautions were still necessary, but all that day we were watched by a large and admiring crowd.

What appeared to strike them most was the smart appearance of the men and the condition of the horses. It seemed to them incredible that men could go into action with polished boots, clean spurs, white lanyards, and with their saddlery clean and their bits and buckles shining. I must say that the men really did look nice that day; the amusing thing was that they knew they were being admired and carried themselves accordingly.

Snipe was inclined to be a bit shabby, so I sent him off into a house, whence he returned with boots like a looking-glass and waxed moustaches. Everywhere I heard the same remark: "*Comme Ils sont propres!*"

No one was prouder than I. It may sound conceited, but I derived great satisfaction from knowing that they were admired.

That evening we withdrew to Douvrain. We passed close to Mons, which was all lighted up and had bands playing in it. I had three men who had seen it in 1914; I wondered what their feeling were when they saw it again after four years! It seemed incredible that here we were at Mons, the place which had always looked so far away on the map. But it was true enough. Canadians were actually in the town, and all kinds of rockets and flares were going up from it.

As for myself, I was not sorry that the war was over, but I could not help having one feeling of regret, and that was that I was never again to lead my troop into the field. After all the trouble I had taken with my corporals, men, horses, etc., it seemed a pity that we were not to start a real pursuit right into Germany. I felt like that at the time, but only for a few hours afterwards.

Chapter 22

After the Armistice—on the Rhine

The result of the Armistice was at first to cheer people up immensely. But this feeling lasted only a very short time. It soon gave way to a strong reaction which seemed to plunge every one into the depths of depression. Rumours began to circulate about the long time that demobilisation would take. Some said that no one would get home for more than a year.

A civilian would have been astonished to see the difference in men's spirits before and after the Armistice. While the war was on you always had felt a kind of stimulus to work hard and do with your might whatever you had to do. But now it was very different. Everyone felt that he had nothing more to look forward to: and to my mind the great essential of happiness is to be always working for some definite object.

A few weeks before we had been training hard for the war of movement, which we knew was coming. Everyone was as keen as mustard. The officers showed it; the men showed it in their whole bearing. People even used to "argue the point" about tactical problems; the whole atmosphere was one of energy.

Some minor incidents go to show what I mean. Corporal Greatorex was rather full of himself after the St. Amand show: I noticed it in several ways. To start with, when we were in billets at Bouvignies about October 28th, he suddenly seemed to have about fifty *per cent*, more energy than he had had a fortnight before. His section, which was in a farm by itself, was beautifully arranged. All his saddlery was magnificently polished, and his swords and rifles, etc., all systematically put up. Now a man does not do this kind of thing of his own accord unless he takes a pride in his work and in himself. Corporal Greatorex always was smart, but he was ten times smarter now. Even the least smart of the men seemed to "buck" themselves up.

A week after the Armistice was declared all this seemed to go by the board. The men became flat, dull, and didn't seem to care about anything. During the march through Belgium our rations were bad, which made things worse. The paucity of supplies could not be helped, and was solely due to the wholesale destruction which the Huns had wrought in the country through which our lines of communication now ran. Everything had to be brought up by motor-lorry instead of rail. This period was one of the most difficult of the whole war.

It is not easy to keep a lot of men amused; but to do so is as important as it is difficult. Horses had to be looked after just the same, often with a greatly diminished number of men, for the regiments were gradually being demobilized or going on leave.

I did not enjoy the march through Belgium. We thought at first that we were going to the Rhine, but before we had gone very far, we heard we were only going as far as Spa. The thought of being billeted on the Rhine appeared to amuse the men considerably; but even this prospect soon faded away from us.

When we settled down near Spa, the education scheme started. Classes were formed for the study of English, French, Mathematics, History, and many technical trades. I used to take classes in French and History every evening. It was very amusing. The trouble is that so many men have forgotten the English Grammar which they learned at school, and the result is that you have to start with English first. At the end of each lesson I use to read aloud the *The Exploits of Brigadier Gerard or the Memoirs of Baron de Marbot*. These are stories which appeal to cavalrymen, and seemed to be appreciated. (*The Life of the Real Brigadier Gerard* volumes 1 & 2 by Jean-Baptise de Marbot are also published by Leonaur.)

One day by way of a diversion I had my troop photographed,

a proceeding which caused much amusement amongst the on-lookers. I noticed, however, that all the other three troops had themselves photographed soon afterwards. I had the whole troop done first mounted and then each section separately. The men were splendidly turned out, and their "parade" that day was the best I have seen for a very long time. Of course, they all sent a photograph home to their sweethearts and wives. Not the least humorous part of the proceedings was when Sergeant Hine's horse tried to lie down at the critical moment.

I have said in another chapter that there is heaps for an officer to do in billets if he is to do his job properly, especially as regards the men's health, cleanliness and amusements. This was doubly important now since the men had little to do except look after the horses, and time was often heavy on their hands. This is the time when things get slack if you are not very careful. Not the least important of a subaltern's duties is to see that every one of his men has a bath each week when circumstances permit, and also a clean change of washing. Every Saturday I used to inspect all the washing, take note of any deficiencies, and see that the proper indents went in.

It may seem rather absurd to the civilian mind to have to do this kind of thing, but one learns from experience that all work in the army must be organised and supervised. I used to make the men bring everything on parade, drawers, socks, shirt, and towel. This is the only way you really get to know what they have got. It is no good asking them, as they always say that they have got things when they haven't. I suppose they are afraid that they will be cursed for not having the things.

By frequent inspections and by signing the indents myself I usually managed to keep them fairly well supplied with kit. It would make civilians smile to see an officer inspecting socks, etc., and telling the men to get them darned when they are full of holes.

Our division was not one of those detailed for the occupation of Germany, but I had occasion soon after Christmas to go to Cologne. Naturally I was intensely interested in what I saw there, for who would not be. Not the least interesting part of the business was crossing the frontier at Welkenraedt. The actual border line here is a road. It seems hard to realise that here you can stand with one foot in Belgium and the other in Germany. There is a house near the place where I crossed over, which stands partly in Belgium and partly in France. On one side it has written up "*Chambres pour Voyageurs*," and on the other, "*Zimmer für Reisende*." Of course, the Belgians here will not have anything to do with the Huns just over the way.

The country over the German frontier is very different from Eastern Belgium. The first few miles of German territory look just like a piece of midland hunting country, being almost all grass, and then the country becomes cultivated and is as flat as a pancake for miles. Between the frontier and Aachen, you see one vast stretch of arable land dotted with villages, each surrounded by trees.

From each you can see the church spire above the tree-tops. This scene reminded me forcibly of the villages of Picardy, where the vast rolling plains are similarly dotted with small villages each hidden by orchards and small woods. The plain before my eyes was full of farmers busy on the land. There seemed to be plenty of horses, though many of the agricultural machines were drawn by bullocks. Another thing I noticed was the large proportion of women amongst the labourers: great strapping, muscular women, too. The crops which I saw seemed to be flourishing and the land itself appeared to be rich.

In this vast agricultural plain, there was not a sign of war: not a soldier, either German or British, was to be seen. Some of the labourers had on old uniforms with ordinary buttons, British *puttees*, and civilian hats. In the villages no one seemed to take much notice of us; at any rate they showed no hostility. The men raised their caps to our officers, and railway, police, and other officials saluted with noticeable smartness.

Beyond Aachen the country is again flat as far as Duren, and even between this town and Cologne there is little change in the scenery, except that there the country is dotted with biggish woods.

What strikes you when you approach Cologne is the enormous number of churches in the place. The town seems to have a spire every few yards. Naturally it is the great double spire of the cathedral that attracts the eye, for it is of tremendous height, and seems to dwarf all the others. Cologne is certainly an imposing spectacle from a distance.

I found it hard to realise when I entered the town that here I was in Germany's foremost Rhine-town, and within a few yards of the Rhine itself. I went down to the river bank and quietly hummed to myself "We've wound up the watch on the Rhine."

It seemed to me almost incredible that here I was actually on the banks of the great river. The crossing of the Rhine had always seemed such a remote possibility, and yet here we were in Cologne in force. I believe we have about 25,000 troops in the town. I wonder how many people really thought that we should one day occupy the place. You can hardly believe your eyes when you see written up "R.T.O. on No. 1 Platform" in the great echoing station, besides sundry notices to officers and other ranks of the British Army. There are, of course, dozens of *Bekanntmachungen* to the civilian population signed "D. Haig," or "Charles Fergusson," or "Herbert Plumer," dealing with the movements of civilians after certain hours, etc., but on the whole life seems to be almost normal.

There were any quantity of brilliantly-lighted shops of all kinds, big shops, too, like Swan and Edgar, or Dickins and Jones, and the goods displayed seemed to be of the most expensive kind. I saw fur coats at sixteen hundred *marks*, and all kinds of costly clothes. One thing that struck me was the quantity of hat shops of the first order, there are several that would rival Lincoln and Bennett or Henry Heath or Scott. Every kind of hat was displayed from "toppers" to Homburgs. Of course, the goods were expensive, for instance, the price of Homburgs was about fifty *marks*. There were some fine hosiers' shops, too, which would make Turnbull and Asser, or Hilditch and Key green with envy. But, although all the German goods looked very nice, they were really very flimsy. I had occasion to buy a pair of braces:

they broke the first time I got on to my horse. I bought a walking stick; this also smashed the first time I leaned on it.

Another thing that struck me was the quantity of people that you saw about. There seemed to be thousands of young fellows about twenty years old or just over. I was told that a lot had been discharged from the army, but that a great many were medically unfit. On the whole, however, the people had a healthy appearance. I did not see many of the proverbially portly, beer-drinking, pipe-smoking Boches. Nearly all the ones I saw were remarkably erect and smart. The railway officials and police being all ex-soldiers were remarkably neat. You saw a fair number of maimed about the streets, and strangely enough the dozen or so that I saw seemed to be all young fellows of nineteen or thereabouts.

One Sunday evening I walked down the Hohestrasse. Sunday evening is the time when all Boches are abroad. The Hohestrasse was simply packed. One could hardly move for the crush. It was just as if a battalion of men and women mixed was marching down the street eight deep. Amongst the civilians our khaki was of course very predominant: there were hundreds of our men walking about too. The civilians seemed to be quite accustomed to them. I wondered what Thomas Atkins thought of Cologne, and Cologne of Thomas Atkins. The women were remarkably neatly dressed. I saw hardly any shabby ones amongst them. Nearly all were in some kind of dark costume; black was the dominating colour, as I suppose it is in all crowds, but of actual mourning I saw little or none.

It was a surprise for anyone to go into an hotel then. All the managers and hall-porters speak English just as in pre-war days. There seemed to be just as many English-speaking waiters as in 1914. During lunch at the *Dom Hof* I asked one where he had been and what he had done during the war.

"I have been three and a half years in the army," he said, "and have been in France, Belgium, and Russia."

"Have you been in action against the British?"

"Yes, sir, I was at Ypres in 1916, and have been at Hulluch and many other places on your front."

"Where were you last autumn?"

"Round Courtrai. I took part in our retreat to the Rhine after the Armistice; we marched the whole way from Courtrai to Aachen."

"Is it true that the discipline of the German Army failed towards the end?"

"No, not in our division. In our regiment especially we had excellent officers and a very high *esprit de corps*."

"But did it fail generally?"

"It did in some places: I saw some things happen which I could never repeat."

"What about the demobilisation of the German Army?"

"Everything was working all right when I left. A lot of men were disarmed by the Soldiers and Workmen's Councils at Aachen as soon as we arrived, and there were, of course, cases of men deserting when they were told that they would have to wait a week to get their papers. I was, however, demobilised in three days. Generally speaking, everything worked very smoothly in this district; of course, I do not know what went on in other parts of Germany."

"What was the moral like in the German Army?"

"Well, sir, it certainly decreased enormously during the retreat, but it never collapsed altogether. The worst time was after the Armistice, when the men only wanted to get home and be demobilised."

Everyone knows the difference in men's spirits in advance and in retreat. I saw this myself in March, 1918.

You could get, even at that time, quite a respectable meal in Cologne. For breakfast you could have bacon and occasionally fried potatoes, though the serving of these was not really allowed; also jam, coffee, saccharine and a kind of sponge cake. There was no bread or butter, and they had not seen the colour of an egg for months. For other meals you could get soup, beef or mutton, chicken, salad and carrots, or cabbage. The price was, of course, fixed by the British Governor. You could buy excellent white wine from six to ten *francs* a bottle. I saw hardly any signs of distress.

The *cafés* seemed to be frequented just as in peace-time. At certain hours you could see the Huns sitting round the little round tables, each with his foaming tankard of beer and each smoking his pipe or cigar. Round every third or fourth table would be British Tommies, each likewise with his foaming tankard looking curiously at the Boches around him.

From the remarks I heard I judged that it was the shape of the Hun's head that our men objected to most. I heard them compared to pear-drops and other articles of various shapes.

A cavalry patrol on the river bank seemed to arouse a great deal of interest. The Boche had great admiration for our horses, and quite a crowd used to collect to see them.

Fancy British troops on the Rhine!

I had to rub my eyes at first to make sure that I was not dreaming, but there was no mistake about it, for there in front of me was Army Headquarters with two stalwart Guardsmen at the door, and the Union Jack floating majestically overhead.

Conclusion

I have tried in the foregoing chapters to give some idea of the life of the cavalry in France. A lot has been written about life in the trenches and about the infantry, both in billets and in action. My object has been not so much to tell of hairbreadth escapes and breathless moments, but to tell of the British cavalryman, his life out there and the relations between officers and men as I saw it myself for thirty-eight months.

During the time I was out there I saw many great changes. When I first joined, many of the officers in the regiment had been in the army before the war. All were regulars from Sandhurst, special reserve, or recently joined from the Varsity. The drain on our supply of officers had not as yet been heavy: later on, however, they had to be almost entirely replaced. Stephens was wounded twice, Davidson was hit, and on his return was appointed adjutant, many more were killed and wounded, and after the German offensive of March, 1918, there was hardly anyone in the regiment whom I had known in 1915.

But the classes from whom our officers were usually taken in peace-time are not limitless. The drain soon became so heavy that very large numbers were promoted from the ranks of other regiments. At first there was a tendency to look askance at many of these. People had not realised that a man can be a gentleman in the best sense of the word without having an income of £500 a year, and without being educated at Eton or Harrow or some first-class public school. I have stated in an early chapter that all that matters in war is whether you are able to lead men.

To do this successfully, you must have the instincts of a gentleman in its best sense, that is, know how to treat human beings, be kind but firm, and have a strong mind of your own. If men think that you understand them and study their interests, that you are a man of sound judgment, and will lead them boldly and sensibly in the field, you can do anything with them. The man who can hold them and get the best out of them must necessarily fulfil the above conditions, and that man has nine-tenths of what is required. If you can do these things, it does not matter whether the cigarettes which you smoke are Sullivan and Powell's or Goldflake, or whether your breeches are made at a West-End tailor or by a less fashionable establishment.

I believe an officer is all the better for being smartly dressed; I do not mean flashily dressed with gaudy breeches, etc., for to my mind the simpler a man's clothes are the better, but there is a great difference between a man who cares what he looks like and one who does not. An officer who does not care about his appearance cannot justly expect his men to care about theirs.

An episode which marked an epoch in the history of our squadron was the passing of Stephens, and the coming of our new skipper in December, 1917. Stephens had been strict and exigent, while the skipper, although conscientious enough, cared nought for smartness, clean turn-out and the like. He got good work out of the squadron, but his methods were the exact reverse of the principles inculcated into us by Stephens. Of course, it must not be forgotten that our recruits towards the end were conscripts, and different material from that which Stephens had been given to train and handle. We received numbers of elderly men who could not be expected to carry themselves like young fellows in their twenties.

The skipper possessed an almost uncanny dislike for anyone who was or had been on a headquarters-staff. Regimental, Brigade, Divisional and Corps Headquarters he regarded as institutions created solely for the oppression of the regimental soldier, and especially of himself and his command. I believe that he assumed that the moment a subaltern was taken away, perhaps temporarily, for any such employment, the unfortunate fellow immediately became a waster, losing all sympathy with his fellow-men. When anyone came back to the squadron after a period of duty, say on Regimental Headquarters, the skipper was inclined to view him with distrust, a fact which caused no little grief amongst those who did their job conscientiously, whatever they were called upon to do.

This, coupled with an almost uncanny addiction to the consumption of charcoal-biscuits and chocolates, was the skipper's chief failing. As a squadron leader he was in many respects ideal. Astonishingly brave in action, clear-headed and cool in a tight corner, he aroused the admiration of those who served with him. He had a wealth of experience, gained on many fronts, and in the early part of the war in a cavalry fight on the Indian frontier, he had cut his way singlehanded through a horde of fanatical tribesmen. Of a kind and sympathetic nature, he drew all towards him; and those who had their heart in their work, as he had, knew that in him they had a staunch friend. He cared nothing for social position, wealth or descent, but looked only on the character and the actions of his troop leaders; for, as he said, by their deeds shall ye know them. Above all, when he told us to get something done, he would leave us to do it in our own way, which is the secret of success as a commander.

But I have finished now. The hurly-burly is done, the battle won, and I find myself at home in a Yorkshire garden, where a spreading sycamore tree affords me welcome shelter from the August sun. As I write these lines, my mind wanders back to those times of two, three, and four years ago. I seem to see again the bustle of bivouacs at dawn, the campfires, and the rain-sodden horse-lines. I see the old squadron on the march once more, with the dapper little Stephens or the old skipper at its head, the latter clad in his old cloak and with his haversack full of those infernal charcoal-biscuits.

I hear again the crash of the German barrage as we thundered down the hill to Wancourt in the snow; and the whistle of the bomb which destroyed my entire troop of horses. I seem to lie once more upon that fatal crest before Amiens, where only the then line of the 2nd Cavalry Division lay between the Huns and the cathedral spire eleven kilometres behind us. It is all done now and we live in a different world.

The skipper has taken unto himself a wife who, it is hoped, will speedily cure him of eating charcoal and chocolates. The old squadron is scattered to the four winds never to be reassembled; but surely each one of us in these days of unrest, strikes and rumours of strikes, wars and rumours of wars, must sometimes, when he sits over his evening fire, cast his memory back to the time when envy, hatred and malice disappeared from amongst us, and all classes were united in the bond of good fellowship.

LEONAUR

ALSO FROM LEONAUR

AVAILABLE IN SOFTCOVER OR HARDCOVER WITH DUST JACKET

THE FALL OF THE MOGHUL EMPIRE OF HINDUSTAN *by H. G. Keene*—By the beginning of the nineteenth century, as British and Indian armies under Lake and Wellesley dominated the scene, a little over half a century of conflict brought the Moghul Empire to its knees.

LADY SALE'S AFGHANISTAN *by Florentia Sale*—An Indomitable Victorian Lady's Account of the Retreat from Kabul During the First Afghan War.

THE CAMPAIGN OF MAGENTA AND SOLFERINO 1859 *by Harold Carmichael Wylly*—The Decisive Conflict for the Unification of Italy.

FRENCH'S CAVALRY CAMPAIGN *by J. G. Maydon*—A Special Correspondent's View of British Army Mounted Troops During the Boer War.

CAVALRY AT WATERLOO *by Sir Evelyn Wood*—British Mounted Troops During the Campaign of 1815.

THE SUBALTERN *by George Robert Gleig*—The Experiences of an Officer of the 85th Light Infantry During the Peninsular War.

NAPOLEON AT BAY, 1814 *by F. Loraine Petre*—The Campaigns to the Fall of the First Empire.

NAPOLEON AND THE CAMPAIGN OF 1806 *by Colonel Vachée*—The Napoleonic Method of Organisation and Command to the Battles of Jena & Auerstädt.

THE COMPLETE ADVENTURES IN THE CONNAUGHT RANGERS *by William Grattan*—The 88th Regiment during the Napoleonic Wars by a Serving Officer.

BUGLER AND OFFICER OF THE RIFLES *by William Green & Harry Smith*—With the 95th (Rifles) during the Peninsular & Waterloo Campaigns of the Napoleonic Wars.

NAPOLEONIC WAR STORIES *by Sir Arthur Quiller-Couch*—Tales of soldiers, spies, battles & sieges from the Peninsular & Waterloo campaingns.

CAPTAIN OF THE 95TH (RIFLES) *by Jonathan Leach*—An officer of Wellington's sharpshooters during the Peninsular, South of France and Waterloo campaigns of the Napoleonic wars.

RIFLEMAN COSTELLO *by Edward Costello*—The adventures of a soldier of the 95th (Rifles) in the Peninsular & Waterloo Campaigns of the Napoleonic wars.